POP
SCIENCE

POP SCIENCE

Serious Answers
to Deep Questions
Posed in Songs

JAMES BALL

TEN SPEED PRESS
California | New York

For Mel,
who knows why

Text copyright © 2018 by James Ball

Published in the United States by Ten Speed Press, an imprint of Random House, a division of Penguin Random House LLC, New York.
www.crownpublishing.com
www.tenspeed.com

Ten Speed Press and the Ten Speed Press colophon are registered trademarks of Penguin Random House LLC.

Originally published in the United Kingdom in 2018 by Boxtree, an imprint of Pan Macmillan, as *Should I Stay or Should I Go?*

Library of Congress Cataloging-in-Publication Data
Names: Ball, James, (Journalist), author.
Title: Pop science : serious answers to deep questions posed in songs / James Ball.
Description: First American edition. | New York : Ten Speed Press, 2019.
Identifiers: LCCN 2019005364 | ISBN 9781984856265 (hardcover)
Subjects: LCSH: Popular culture—Humor. | Popular music—Humor.
Classification: LCC PN6231.P635 B36 2019 | DDC 818/.602—dc23 LC record
  available at https://lccn.loc.gov/2019005364

Hardcover ISBN: 978-1-9848-5626-5
eBook ISBN: 978-1-9848-5627-2

Printed in the United States of America

Cover design by Chloe Rawlins
Cover illustration by Morrison 1977
Design and illustrations by James Edgar Design

10 9 8 7 6 5 4 3 2 1

First American Edition

CONTENTS

ACKNOWLEDGMENTS ix

**HOW MANY ROADS MUST
A MAN WALK DOWN?**
BOB DYLAN 1

CAN YOU KILL SOMEONE WITH A SONG?
ROBERTA FLACK 2

**ARE THERE 4,000 HOLES IN
BLACKBURN, LANCASHIRE?**
THE BEATLES 4

**HOW MUCH IS THAT DOGGIE
IN THE WINDOW?**
PATTI PAGE 7

DO THEY KNOW IT'S CHRISTMAS TIME?
BAND AID 9

HOW SOON IS NOW?
THE SMITHS 11

CAN I KICK IT?
A TRIBE CALLED QUEST 12

**HOW LONG DOES IT TAKE TO
APOLOGIZE A TRILLION TIMES?**
OUTKAST 14

**VOULEZ-VOUS COUCHER
AVEC MOI CE SOIR?**
LADY MARMALADE, LABELLE ET AL. 16

WHO RUN THE WORLD?
BEYONCÉ 19

IS THIS BURNING AN ETERNAL FLAME?
THE BANGLES 20

WAR—HUH—WHAT IS IT GOOD FOR?
EDWIN STARR 23

**HOW LIKELY IS RIHANNA
TO NEED HER UMBRELLA?**
RIHANNA 24

**IS THIS THE REAL LIFE?
IS THIS JUST FANTASY?**
QUEEN 27

ARE YOU CALLING ME "DARLING"?
THE TING TINGS 28

**HOW MUCH WOULD IT
TAKE TO CRY A RIVER?**
VARIOUS ARTISTS 31

WHERE HAVE ALL THE FLOWERS GONE?
PETER, PAUL, AND MARY 32

SHOULD I STAY OR SHOULD I GO?
THE CLASH 35

**DOES YOUR MOTHER KNOW
THAT YOU'RE OUT?**
ABBA 36

DO YOU GIVE ME FEVER?
PEGGY LEE   39

WHAT WOULDN'T MEAT LOAF DO?
MEAT LOAF   40

ARE FRIENDS ELECTRIC?
GARY NUMAN   43

**HOW DO YOU SOLVE
A PROBLEM LIKE MARIA?**
THE SOUND OF MUSIC   44

**HOW MANY GENERATIONS WILL
HAVE PASSED BY THE YEAR 3000?**
BUSTED   47

WHEN WILL I BE FAMOUS?
BROS   48

ARE WE HUMAN, OR DANCER?
THE KILLERS   51

**YOU WALK 500 MILES.
YOU WALK 500 MORE.
WHERE HAVE YOU BEEN?**
THE PROCLAIMERS   52

WHERE IS MY LARGE AUTOMOBILE?
TALKING HEADS   55

**DID THOSE FEET IN ANCIENT TIMES WALK
UPON ENGLAND'S MOUNTAINS GREEN?**
WILLIAM BLAKE   56

ARE WE OUT OF THE WOODS YET?
TAYLOR SWIFT   59

I WILL SURVIVE—BUT FOR HOW LONG?
GLORIA GAYNOR   60

**IF YOU DON'T LOVE ME NOW,
WILL YOU NEVER LOVE ME AGAIN?**
FLEETWOOD MAC   63

**HOW MUCH SPACE DO A MILLION
PHOTOGRAPHS TAKE UP?**
THE VAPORS   64

IS ANNIE OKAY?
MICHAEL JACKSON   67

**HOW MANY HONEYS
MAKE THEIR MONEY?**
DESTINY'S CHILD   68

IS SHE REALLY GOING OUT WITH HIM?
JOE JACKSON   71

WILL THIS BE THE DAY THAT YOU DIE?
DON MCLEAN   72

CAN YOU FEEL THE LOVE TONIGHT?
ELTON JOHN AND TIM RICE   75

CALL ME, MAYBE?
CARLY RAE JEPSEN   76

**WERE THE BOYS OF THE NYPD
CHOIR SINGING "GALWAY BAY"?**
THE POGUES   79

IS MONEY THE ROOT OF ALL EVIL TODAY?
PINK FLOYD   80

WHY DON'T WE DO IT IN THE ROAD?
THE BEATLES   83

DO THE DRUGS WORK?
THE VERVE   84

ARE THERE NINE MILLION
BICYCLES IN BEIJING?
KATIE MELUA 87

DO YOU KNOW THE WAY TO SAN JOSÉ?
DIONNE WARWICK 89

HOW WORRIED SHOULD YOU BE IF
SOMEONE'S WATCHING YOU WITH
THE EYE OF THE TIGER?
SURVIVOR 90

WOULD I LIE TO YOU?
CHARLES & EDDIE 93

HOW MUCH WOULD YOU HAVE
TO EARN TO BE "BARELY GETTIN' BY"
IN LA IN 1980?
DOLLY PARTON 94

WHAT BECOMES OF THE BROKENHEARTED?
JIMMY RUFFIN 97

WHO'S TO BLAME: THE SUNSHINE,
MOONLIGHT, GOOD TIMES, OR BOOGIE?
THE JACKSONS 98

ARE YOU TELLING ME THIS IS A SIGN?
SNOOP DOGG 100

AM I A CREEP?
RADIOHEAD 102

DID WE USED TO KNOW
WHITE CHRISTMASES?
BING CROSBY 105

WHAT ABOUT ELEPHANTS—
HAVE WE LOST THEIR TRUST?
MICHAEL JACKSON 107

WHAT COMPARES TO YOU?
SINEAD O'CONNOR 109

DO YOU LIKE PIÑA COLADAS, AND
GETTING CAUGHT IN THE RAIN?
RUPERT HOLMES 110

ARE YOU LONESOME TONIGHT?
ELVIS PRESLEY 113

WHAT DOES THE FOX SAY?
YLVIS 114

ISN'T IT IRONIC, DON'T YOU THINK?
ALANIS MORISSETTE 117

WHAT IS LOVE?
HADDAWAY 118

WILL IT BE LONELY THIS CHRISTMAS?
MUD 121

WHY'D YOU HAVE TO GO AND
MAKE THINGS SO COMPLICATED?
AVRIL LAVIGNE 122

WHERE ARE YOUR FRIENDS TONIGHT?
LCD SOUNDSYSTEM 125

WHAT'S COOLER THAN BEING COOL?
OUTKAST 126

WHY DO YOU ONLY CALL ME
WHEN YOU'RE HIGH?
ARCTIC MONKEYS 129

WHERE IS 24 HOURS FROM TULSA?
GENE PITNEY 130

OH CAN'T YOU SEE YOU BELONG TO ME?
THE POLICE   133

WHAT'S THE FREQUENCY, KENNETH?
REM   134

DO GIRLS JUST WANNA HAVE FUN?
CYNDI LAUPER   137

WHERE DO BROKEN HEARTS GO?
WHITNEY HOUSTON   138

WHAT HAVE THEY DONE TO THE RAIN?
THE SEARCHERS   141

SON, CAN YOU PLAY ME A MEMORY?
BILLY JOEL   142

WHY?
ANNIE LENNOX   145

DOES EVERYBODY WANT TO RULE THE WORLD?
TEARS FOR FEARS   146

HOW MANY INCHES ARE IN A MILE?
SELENA GOMEZ & THE SCENE   148

HAVE GUILTY FEET GOT NO RHYTHM?
WHAM   150

HOW THE HELL AM I SUPPOSED TO LEAVE?
USHER   153

IS THERE LIFE ON MARS?
DAVID BOWIE   154

WHAT'S GOING ON?
4 NON BLONDES   157

WHO LET THE DOGS OUT?
BAHA MEN   158

IS THIS SONG ABOUT YOU?
CARLY SIMON   161

WHAT WOULD HAPPEN IF IT WERE CHRISTMAS EVERY DAY?
WIZZARD   162

WHY DO BIRDS SUDDENLY APPEAR?
THE CARPENTERS   165

WHAT IF GOD WAS ONE OF US?
JOAN OSBORNE   166

WHY DOES IT ALWAYS RAIN ON ME?
TRAVIS   169

WHO DO YOU THINK YOU ARE?
SPICE GIRLS   170

DO YOU REMEMBER THE FIRST TIME?
PULP   173

WHO STARTED THE FIRE?
BILLY JOEL   174

A NOTE ON CITATIONS   176

SONG CREDITS   177

ACKNOWLEDGMENTS

This book owes its existence to Nicky Woolf, whose late-night drunken attempt to fact-check "Ms. Jackson" on Twitter sparked a correction from me. In turn, that prompted then editor at BuzzFeed Janine Gibson to make me turn it into an article, which prompted Boxtree editor Jamie Coleman to suggest this book.

Thanks are due to everyone at Pan Macmillan, and especially to James Edgar, whose brilliant illustrations are throughout the book. Thanks are also due to Luke, Caroline, Holly, Tom, David, and others who have input suggestions throughout. Thanks also to the team at Ten Speed Press: Lisa, Aaron, Chloe, Kristin, Daniel, and Dan. All errors remain entirely my fault.

Serious credit and apologies are due to every artist whose work I've butchered in this work—thank you all for posing so many great questions.

Finally, I would like to single out Mel's friend Alice, who was absolutely no help at all.

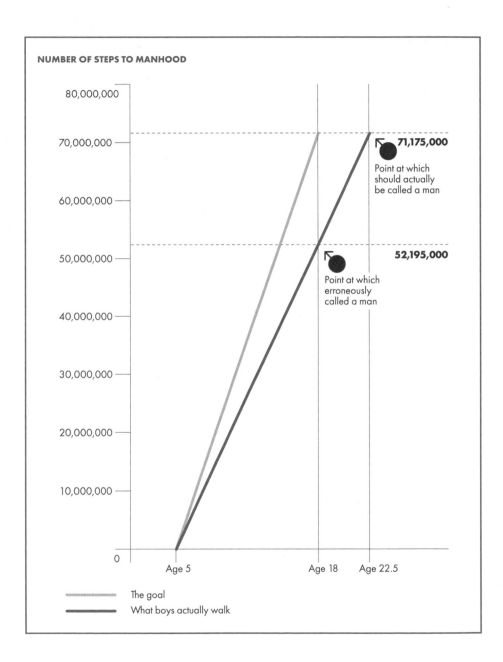

NUMBER OF STEPS TO MANHOOD

80,000,000

71,175,000
Point at which
should actually
be called a man

70,000,000

60,000,000

52,195,000

Point at which
erroneously
called a man

50,000,000

40,000,000

30,000,000

20,000,000

10,000,000

0

Age 5   Age 18   Age 22.5

········· The goal

——— What boys actually walk

HOW MANY ROADS MUST A MAN WALK DOWN?

BOB DYLAN

There have been various rituals around manhood throughout history: for the Bukusu tribe of western Kenya, it is the sikhebo circumcision ceremony; for the people of Vanuatu in the South Pacific, it is the yearly harvest ritual of "land diving," as they leap a hundred feet from crudely built wooden towers with vines tied around their ankles.

Dylan, B., characteristically chooses an unusual measure of child development, contemplating how many roads a man must walk down, before you can call him a man. Despite significant research effort, we have been unable to find evidenced answers to this matter "blowing in the wind" (unless the cryptic answer to his question is "nitrogen, oxygen, argon, carbon dioxide, and other trace gases") and so have focused instead on what Dylan surely must have been driving at: childhood physical activity.

The lack of any standardized road length, plus ethical (and insurance) considerations, prevented us proposing that young children walk down actual roads, so instead we have focused on recommended step counts for children. While adults are advised to walk 10,000 steps a day, children—at least those aged five or over; for hopefully obvious reasons younger kids are excluded—are advised

to walk more. Girls should be aiming to walk 12,000 steps a day, but boys need to average 15,000 steps each day. Therefore, a simple bit of math suggests a boy should have walked 71,175,000 steps between his fifth and eighteenth birthday, when we can (legally) call him a man. However, most children fall short of this: the average boy will have walked just 52,195,000 steps by this point.

The Dylan, B., study sadly is vague on practical advice on what to do at this point should we wish to maintain our current age of majority. We could either reduce the requirements for roads (or steps) walked down, or, if we wish to protect the 71-million-step goal, we could instead begin to call boys "men" at the average age of just over twenty-two and a half. It is of course likely that this additional exercise would cause them to be blowing in the wind.

CAN YOU KILL SOMEONE WITH A SONG?

ROBERTA FLACK

Flack, R., repeatedly makes a number of serious accusations against an unnamed individual over the course of this report, most notably alleging attempted murder, softly and with a song.

Given the damaging nature of such allegations—they could easily result in lifetime imprisonment—it's important to examine the evidence behind Flack's claim. Initially, Flack's claims stand up well: it is entirely possible to kill someone with a song, or any other appropriately loud noise. Anything over 150 decibels is enough to rupture an eardrum, while anything rising to around 200 decibels is enough to prove fatal to most of us. For comparison, a pneumatic drill is around 100 decibels, and chain saws are only around 120 decibels—to hear a fatal level of noise you'd generally need to be near an explosion.

Flack, however, specifies she is not being killed by volume: her accusation is that she is being softly killed. Here too, though, she may have evidence to support her claims. In 1933, a Hungarian composer penned a song called "Gloomy Sunday," initially about the despair of war, then rewritten to be about contemplating suicide. The song provoked a (badly evidenced) international media panic through the decade that it was provoking a swathe of suicides—and the composer did eventually kill himself, although decades later. An examination of the case of "Gloomy Sunday" in *Gizmodo*—we assume this to be a peer-reviewed journal—noted that Hungary has a historically high suicide rate, as do other countries with its cultural history, leading to speculation about genetic causes of the phenomenon.

The effect of a piece of music or another suicide provoking a copycat act is known as the "Werther Effect," after the 1774 novel *The Sorrows of Young Werther* by Johann Wolfgang von Goethe. The book's eponymous protagonist kills himself over doomed love, and its publication was followed by a spate of suicides, provoking huge debate as to whether they were related.

So, if Flack's lover is softly singing "Gloomy Sunday" into her ears, she may have a good case against him for attempted murder.

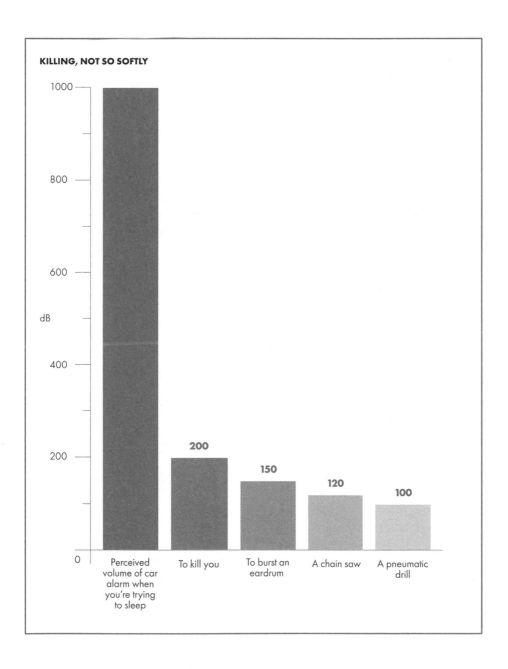

KILLING, NOT SO SOFTLY

dB

- 1000
- 800
- 600
- 400
- 200
- 0

200 — To kill you

150 — To burst an eardrum

120 — A chain saw

100 — A pneumatic drill

Perceived volume of car alarm when you're trying to sleep

ARE THERE 4,000 HOLES IN BLACKBURN, LANCASHIRE?

THE BEATLES

Some thinkers tackle love, some tackle betrayal, and some tackle politics— but few have tackled a pressing issue that causes fury among drivers everywhere: potholes.

Perhaps their willingness to address this issue is why Lennon, J., and McCartney, P., have endured in the public imagination for so long.

In their 1967 address, they not only note that there are 4,000 "small" holes in Blackburn, Lancashire, but also that someone had to count them. Today, trying to assess whether their estimate at the time was accurate is impossible, but it is still the case that someone in contemporary Blackburn has to try to calculate the number of potholes and deal with them.

A recent estimate of potholes in Blackburn can be gathered from the local council's figures. In 2018 the council received £178,000 from a central government fund to tackle potholes. The average cost of fixing a pothole in Britain is £53, which means Blackburn got enough funds to tackle 3,358 potholes—not too far from Lennon and McCartney's historical estimate, especially given that budget measures in Britain mean the council was likely underfunded in its efforts.

It seems like in the case of Lennon and McCartney science's gain may have been road maintenance's loss.

As to how many holes it would take to "fill" the Albert Hall: we know its internal volume measures 113,512 yards, so if all the holes were the same size they would be 28.38 yd.^{3}, which is roughly two-thirds the size of a standard shipping container. It is unlikely that there were 4,000 holes this size in the roads of Blackburn, Lancashire, especially as the study itself says they are "rather small," so though one may have led to the calculation of the other, we must reluctantly conclude that the collaborators may have made some serious errors in their math.

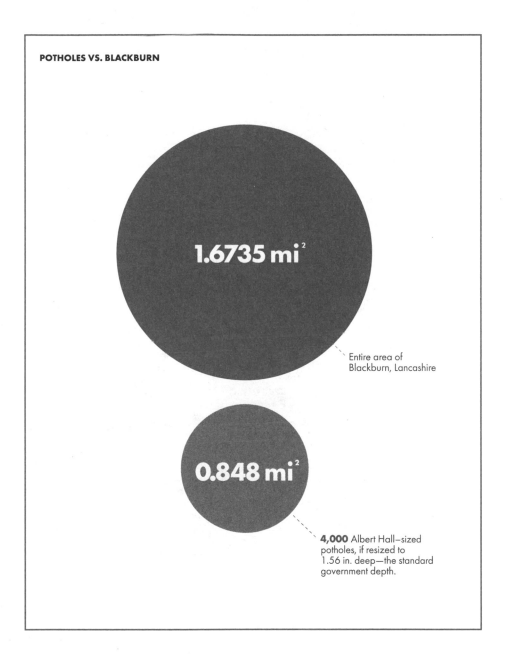

1.6735 mi^2

Entire area of
Blackburn, Lancashire

0.848 mi^2

4,000 Albert Hall–sized
potholes, if resized to
1.56 in. deep—the standard
government depth.

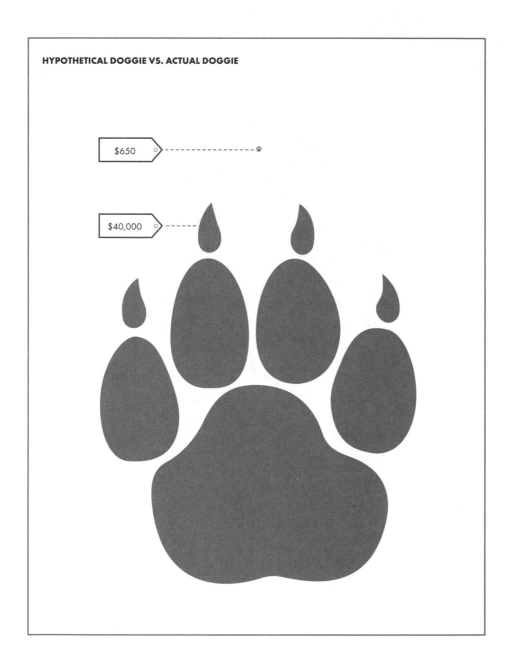

HOW MUCH IS THAT DOGGIE IN THE WINDOW?

PATTI PAGE

There is a serious concern we must address about Page, P.'s, 1953 study of pet economics.

Building upon original research by Merrill, B., we can't avoid the fact that Page is clearly a horribly irresponsible purchaser of pets. Firstly, as numerous charities have tried to teach us, dogs are for life and not just for Christmas; purchasing decisions should not be made on the whim of seeing a dog in a window.

Similarly, to avoid issues of animal cruelty, you should never buy a puppy if you haven't seen it with its mother (in person; photos don't count). Page also seems torn over what she's looking for in a puppy: one moment she's referring to its cute "waggly" tail, the next she says it needs to be a guard dog to keep her lover safe. It's almost as if the missive doesn't want to be taken seriously as a purchasing guide to pets.

That's no reason not to answer the economic question the study poses, of course. If the dog in question is a mongrel, then its purchase price shouldn't be too high, likely not much more than $400 to $700—though if it's pedigree it could cost several thousand off the shelf.

Don't let that price lull you into a false sense of security, though. The People's Dispensary for Sick Animals (PDSA) says that, depending on the size and life span of the dog that you choose, over its lifetime it could set you back between $20,000 and $40,000. In light of this, the short answer to the question is "between 5,000 and 10,000 percent more expensive than you think."

We earnestly ask Ms. Page to undertake much more serious thought before she again ponders whether that dog is for sale.

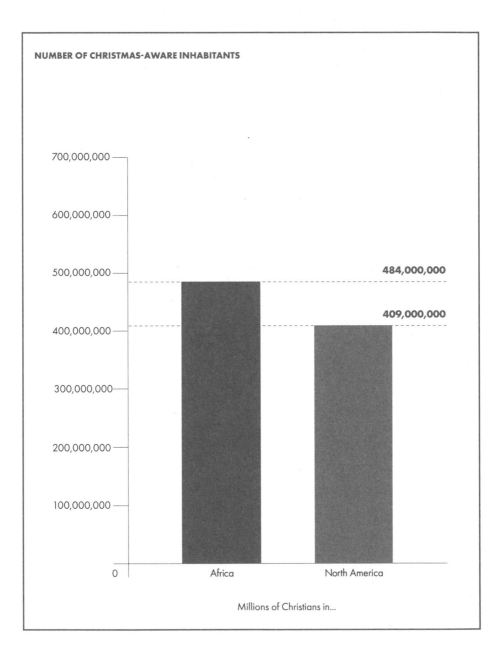

NUMBER OF CHRISTMAS-AWARE INHABITANTS

700,000,000

600,000,000

500,000,000 — — — — — — 484,000,000

409,000,000

400,000,000 — — — — — —

300,000,000

200,000,000

100,000,000

0   Africa   North America

Millions of Christians in...

DO THEY KNOW IT'S CHRISTMAS TIME?

BAND AID

It is somewhat puzzling that large groups of individuals have gathered to ask this question at various points spanning more than three decades, as it is one that is almost trivial to solve.

This question was first posed as part of a huge charity drive in 1984 and was collectively sung by no fewer than thirty-seven vocalists, who seemed very keen to get an answer. However, it was then asked again by a fresh group a few years later, and a third and fourth time by different groups in 2004 and 2014, in each instance focused on the continent of Africa.

On the face of it, answering this question is very simple: the latest estimates suggest that Africa has a Christian population of nearly 500 million out of a total population of 1.2 billion, meaning that even if Africans didn't follow the customs of people living on other continents, it's still extremely likely that they have a very good idea indeed that it's Christmas time, as almost every other person is a Christian.

However, if we were to look more specifically at Ethiopia—the initial fund-raising target for the commendable Band Aid initiative—the answer is slightly less clear. Almost two-thirds of Ethiopians, some 45 million people, identify as Christian and so could clearly be expected to know when Christmas is. However, of this figure, more than 30 million identify as Orthodox Christians, meaning they would not celebrate Christmas on the same day as their Protestant or Catholic brethren. This, perhaps, solves the mystery of this question's persistence: clearly, the celebrity fund-raisers have struggled to understand the differences in how various Christian groups in Ethiopia mark Christmas.

One thing that is beyond doubt is that there will be snow in Africa every Christmas. Africa is a huge continent with mountain ranges including Kenya's Mount Kenya, Tanzania's Mount Kilimanjaro, Uganda's Rwenzori Mountains, and, even more specifically for the purposes of this study, Ethiopia's Semien Mountain—all of which are covered in snow for almost the entirety of the year.

Fementosecond	10^{-15}s	Pulse time on fastest lasers.
Svedberg	10^{-13}s	Time unit used for sedimentation rates (usually of proteins).
Picosecond	10^{-12}s	A picosecond is to one second as one second is to approximately 31,689 years.
Nanosecond	10^{-9}s	Time for molecules to fluoresce.
Microsecond	10^{-6}s	Symbol is μs.
Millisecond	0.001s	Shortest time unit used on stopwatches.
Second	1s	SI base unit.
Morrissey	5s	The length of time into reading a contemporary interview with him that fans start to feel a bit sad.

HOW SOON IS NOW?

THE SMITHS

Anyone who's had to sit and wait for a delivery knows just how painful it can be, and so it's not difficult for us to empathize with Marr, J., and Morrissey, S., when they plaintively seek detail on what their interlocutor means when they promise that something is going to happen right now.

Lesser investigators may be willing to just accept "now" as a period of somewhere between two and three seconds, but Marr and Morrissey are clearly not prepared to be fobbed off by such lengthy and vague periods, asking "When exactly do you mean?" They can and should expect a far greater level of precision on just how instantaneous "now" should be. What they are clearly asking is, "What is the soonest that now can be?"

We may have heard of a millisecond, which is one-thousandth of a second, or a microsecond, which is one-millionth of it, but even these are clunky and extended units of time versus "now." We might even start to think about an attosecond—a unit of time so small that it's been noted that an attosecond is to a second what a second is to the entire age of the universe. These things are quick.

But even an attosecond is an eternity compared to the one unit we can really say is "now"—the Planck unit, which is the time it takes for light to travel, well, a really really short distance, and is the smallest possible measure of time (and far smaller than we can measure yet).

So, Marr and Morrissey, how soon is now? It's just a Planck unit away.

CAN I KICK IT?

A TRIBE CALLED QUEST

This is a question that has taxed many thinkers since it was first posed by A Tribe Called Quest in 1990, as it's since been asked again by persons ranging from Jay-Z to Williams, R., among many others.

It's not a surprise that this is a question they feel a need to revisit, as answering it requires us to make use of complex concepts around the laws of consent and the laws of property rights.

As a first principle, if the "it" you're referring to is a living being, you're being rude and should use better pronouns. But in this instance then you absolutely cannot kick "it" in the absence of consent: in kicking a person you could break laws relating to assault and bodily harm. If an animal, then there are welfare rules. If you are considering kicking an adult person with their consent—this is a judgment-free zone—then do it gently as there is a maximum level of harm to which someone can legally consent.

In the circumstance that the "it" under consideration for kicking is an object, things get simpler. You might want to think carefully first if the object is a brick or a glass window, as while you may have a legal right to kick something, that does nothing to help your greatly injured foot.

However, if you own the object, or have rights to use it (and insurance against damage to it), or permission from someone who does—and have checked it's unlikely to cause you harm—then we have good news: yes, you can.

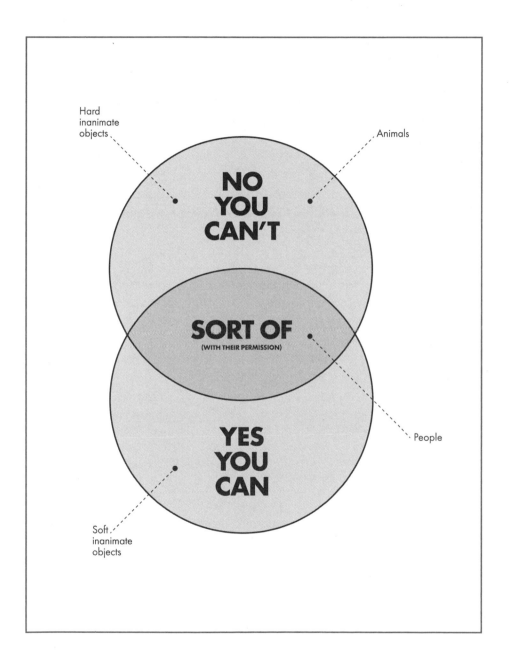

Hard inanimate objects

Animals

NO YOU CAN'T

SORT OF
(WITH THEIR PERMISSION)

People

YES YOU CAN

Soft inanimate objects

HOW LONG DOES IT TAKE TO APOLOGIZE A TRILLION TIMES?

OUTKAST

Relationships are never straightforward, and the relationship between a man and his partner's mother is a notoriously tricky one.

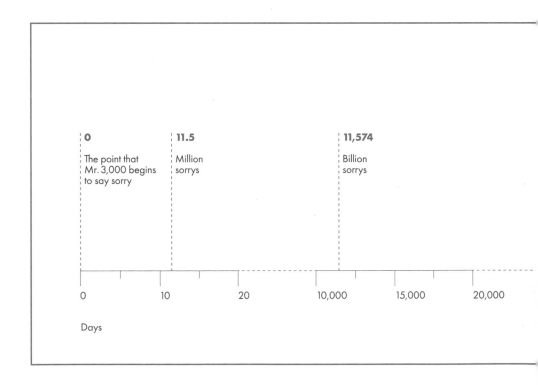

0
The point that Mr. 3,000 begins to say sorry

11.5
Million sorrys

11,574
Billion sorrys

0   10   20   10,000   15,000   20,000

Days

It's commendable, then, that Outkast—and André 3000 in particular—are keen to make amends to Ms. Jackson after problems with her daughter.

Knowing that one apology is never enough, Mr. 3000 repeatedly reassures Ms. Jackson he is so sorry that he apologizes "a trillion times." But new analysis suggests he might not be telling the truth. If we generously assume that Mr. 3000 can say "sorry" once a second, 24 hours a day, with no break, he will after one full year have apologized just 31 million times.

To reach a full trillion apologies, Mr. 3000 will have to continue apologizing once a second, 24/7, for just over 31,688 years. However, at the time of the song's release, he was just over twenty-five years old—meaning that even if he had begun apologizing the moment he was born, he would have said sorry just 775 million times—less than a thousandth of his claimed total of sorrow.

As a result of all that, it seems like we owe Ms. Jackson an apology of our own: we're sorry, but the evidence suggests Mr. 3000 was in fact not for real, after all.

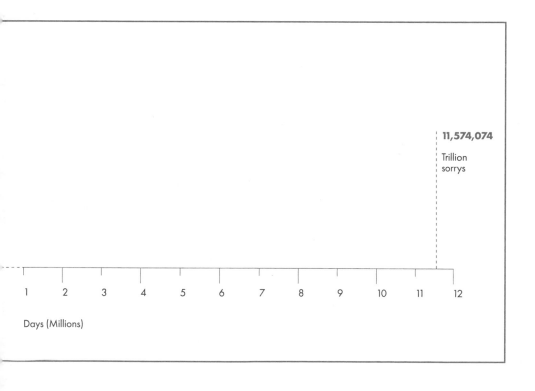

11,574,074

Trillion sorrys

1   2   3   4   5   6   7   8   9   10   11   12

Days (Millions)

VOULEZ-VOUS COUCHER AVEC MOI CE SOIR?

LADY MARMALADE, LABELLE ET AL.

This question has frequently been investigated over the years, and research published in 1989 by two American psychologists, Russell D. Clark and Elaine Hatfield, might help us answer it definitively.

They asked a group of five female students and four male students to approach people of the opposite gender on a college campus, introduce themselves, say they found the stranger attractive, and then ask one of three questions: "Would you go out with me tonight?," "Would you come over to my apartment?," or "Would you go to bed with me?"

For the first question, going on a date, the success rate for both men and women was about the same—a surprisingly high 50 percent (roughly) said they were willing to go on a date with a total stranger. As soon as we shift to the second question—going to an apartment—the success rate with women drops to almost nothing, but with men the success rate jumps to a pleasing 69 percent.

And as for the "Would you go to bed with me tonight?" question, not a single woman in either of the original studies said yes to this question—but almost three-quarters of men did. So, if you want to ask this question and get a positive response, ask a man.

As to why the question is posed in French—a global survey carried out by Durex in 2005 found that the French had an average of 8.1 sexual partners, lower than the global average of 9 and way behind the Turkish, who had an average of 14.5. And though they were above the average of 103 for the number of times they had sex each year, they were still trailing way behind their Greek counterparts, who had sex 138 times a year.

So statistically, if you're looking for the answer to be yes, you're much better off asking *Tha koimitheís mazí mou apópse?* or *Bu gece benimle uyuyacak mısın?*

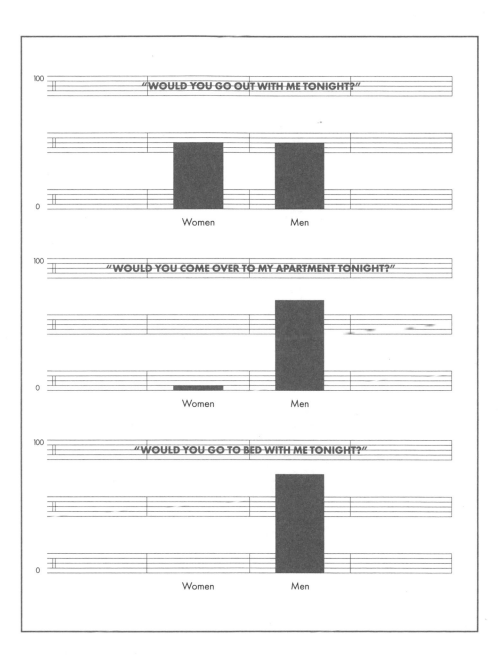

WHO RUNS THE UK'S BUSINESSES?

79% men not called David or Steve

8% David

7% Steve

6% Women

WHO RUN THE WORLD?

BEYONCÉ

No human being takes pleasure in correcting Knowles, B., but alas on this issue we are forced to do so.

Despite the fact that a boy once ascended to become a head of state at the age of six months (Egypt's Fuad II, who took the throne in 1952, only to be deposed eleven months later—before his second birthday), there are few under-eighteens at the top of global politics, and no girls—by which of course we mean women under eighteen—running any country in the world at present.

If the answer isn't "girls," then who does run the world? The answer may disappoint Ms. Knowles, and feminists everywhere, but it probably won't surprise them as it is of course middle-aged men. Of the 193 member states of the UN, at time of writing, only fifteen have a woman serving as head of state or head of government—that's fewer than one in ten. Only around one in three countries analyzed had ever had a female at the top of their politics.

Things don't get any better in the business world: research in 2017 into the UK's hundred biggest companies found there were more major corporations led by men called David (eight) or Stephen (seven) than there were companies led by women (six). Things are no better in the US: in early 2018, only twenty-seven of the USA's 500 biggest companies were led by a woman.

It is not for the authors to judge why this reality was not reflected in Ms. Knowles's published research, but one hypothesis is that it's a bit bleak really.

IS THIS BURNING AN ETERNAL FLAME?

THE BANGLES

This is an important case file of three patients who presented together with a very similar set of symptoms in 1988.

In the interests of patient confidentiality, we shall refer to them by the case name of "The Bangles." These three women reported "burning" that was so persistent as to lead all three to worry at length that the symptoms would proceed persistently, if not eternally.

While explaining their problem, the Bangles encourage their doctor to take their pulse (somewhat oddly with their eyes closed and referring to them as "darling," but this is clearly bound up in their nervousness of the clinical diagnostic process); express hope that someone would be able to ease their pain; and explain their symptoms had been causing loneliness, suggesting the burning sensations were a barrier to normal romantic relationships.

Given the stigma around such conditions, it is perhaps not surprising that the Bangles were willing only to describe their symptoms euphemistically, and that all three were worried the problem would prove insoluble.

However, there are multiple possible diagnoses that bode well for the women: rather than being an eternal flame, the burning experienced by all three is far more likely to be a symptom of thrush—or, given the women are assumed to be sexually active, could be a symptom of treatable STDs such as chlamydia or gonorrhea. All of these infections respond well to the proper treatments, and so the Bangles serve as an excellent example to others of the benefit of seeking early treatment, rather than worrying for too long.

Although their hope that just having a doctor say their name would be enough to banish the symptoms is rather unlikely, we know that often, because of the placebo effect, just having a clinician pay attention can lead to improvements in patients' symptoms. Interestingly, a recent study by doctors at the University of York found that the use of copper bangles for treating arthritic pain "had no statistically significant therapeutic effect among patients."

PERCENTAGE OF WOMEN IN THE US WHO WILL SUFFER FROM THRUSH AT SOME POINT IN THEIR LIVES

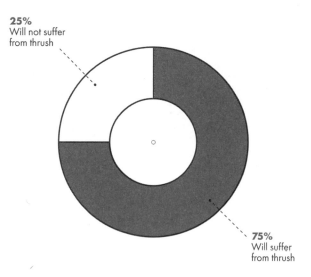

25%
Will not suffer from thrush

75%
Will suffer from thrush

NUMBER OF PEOPLE WHO SUFFERED FROM GONORRHEA, CHLAMYDIA, AND EXTERNAL FLAME-RELATED INJURIES IN THE US IN 2017

555,608
Reported cases of gonorrhea

1,708,569
Reported cases of chlamydia

0
People diagnosed with symptoms relating to eternal flame-related injuries

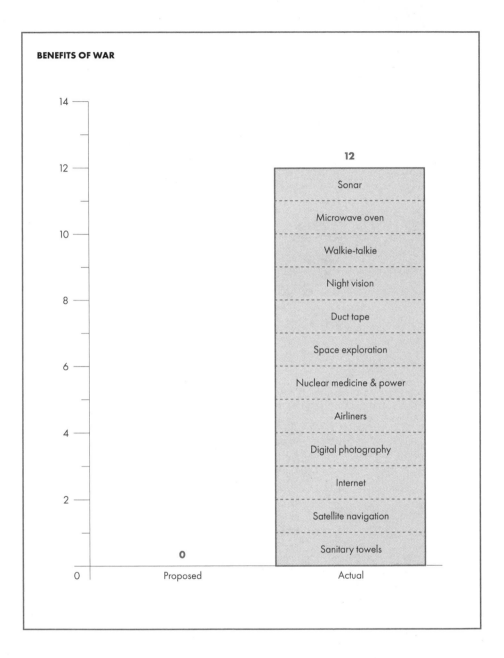

BENEFITS OF WAR

14

12   **12**

Sonar

Microwave oven

10   Walkie-talkie

Night vision

8   Duct tape

Space exploration

6   Nuclear medicine & power

Airliners

4   Digital photography

Internet

2   Satellite navigation

Sanitary towels

0

0   Proposed   Actual

WAR—HUH— WHAT IS IT GOOD FOR?

EDWIN STARR

Starr, E.'s, provocative framing of this question forces us to reassess something the majority of us believe to be a bad thing, which should be avoided at almost any cost, and consider instead its upsides.

As he no doubt expected us to realize, there is a long list of potential good outcomes from war, in the right circumstances.

Firstly, as evidenced in the most extreme case of the Second World War, and more recently in Kosovo, war serves as a backstop against genocidal dictators and helps preserve the rights and freedoms of minorities, and as countries through history have found, war can serve as an effective way of preserving territorial integrity against aggressors.

Additionally, wars—at least in their early days—can serve to hugely boost the popularity of democratically elected leaders. Margaret Thatcher's approval ratings shot from 41 percent to 59 percent in the three months of the Falklands War, while George Bush's ratings leaped from 51 percent to 86 percent following 9/11 and the US's subsequent invasion of Afghanistan.

Research from the State University of New York suggests such gains take a long time to fall back, making it a worthwhile proposition for the leaders. Though the research is out on the long-term economic benefits, it's clear that in the short term it has a positive impact, especially boosting the manufacturing sector.

Mr. Starr would surely, though, also not wish us to forget the inventions that have come out of war—or at least military-backed research—which include the early internet, plastic surgery, superglue, chemotherapy, and even canned food. While we wish Mr. Starr had asked us to consider the horrors of war at greater depth, he does make a compelling case for its upsides.

War—huh—what is it good for? Democracy, political popularity, technology, and the short-term economy.

HOW LIKELY IS RIHANNA TO NEED HER UMBRELLA?

RIHANNA

Fenty, R., would like it to be known she's a supportive friend: she repeatedly makes it clear that while she is there for you when the sun shines, she also intends to be there when it is raining, and will bring an umbrella to shelter you.

Fenty, R., this is to be commended, but if we are to examine how useful Fenty's strategy of umbrella-carrying is in practice, we need to collect some data to see whether or not her approach is effective. This, of course, is complicated by Fenty's move from the city she grew up in—Bridgetown, the capital of Barbados—to Los Angeles.

In Bridgetown, despite the warm weather it rains 153 out of the year's 365 days. So on any given day her umbrella has a 42 percent chance of being useful—meaning she's a friend you would likely be glad to have around for that reason alone.

However, in her new home of Los Angeles the situation is very different: several months of the year average between zero or one day of rain in the month, and across the year there are only typically thirty-seven rainy days. This means that on 89.9 percent of days of the year, Ms. Fenty will be carrying an umbrella for no reason, which may even begin to look eccentric.

As a result, we recommend that Fenty adapt her friendship strategy to better suit the pleasant climate of her new home. We have every confidence in her success.

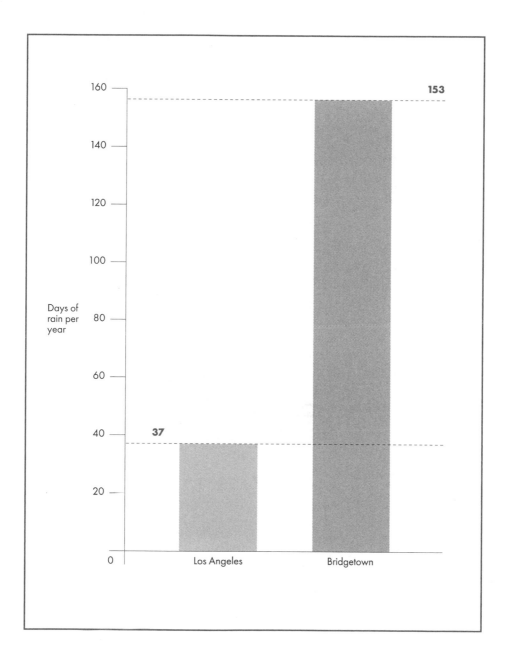

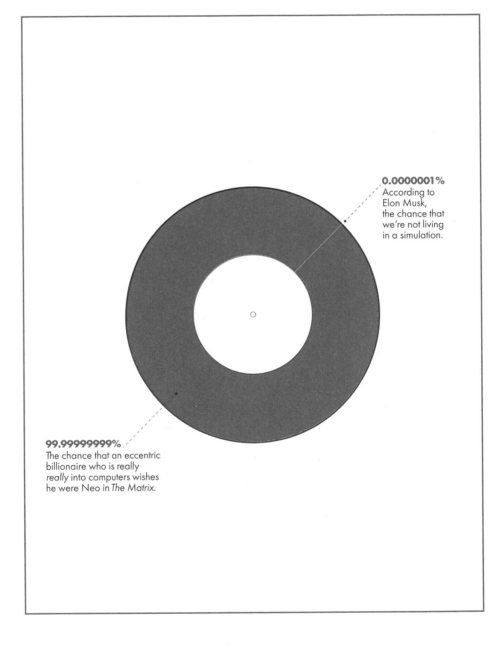

0.0000001%
According to
Elon Musk,
the chance that
we're not living
in a simulation.

99.99999999%
The chance that an eccentric
billionaire who is really
really into computers wishes
he were Neo in *The Matrix*.

IS THIS THE REAL LIFE? IS THIS JUST FANTASY?

QUEEN

Mercury, F., begins his 1975 investigation into the nature of reality by imagining a figure guilty of murder before quickly moving through a dizzying invocation of cultural knowledge, from meteorology to dance, theatre to religion, and whether someone will let someone else go.

This is clearly an early foray on the part of guitarist May, B., into astrophysics, in which he later obtained a PhD from Imperial College, London.

The fields of physics and philosophy have both wondered whether it could be possible that the universe in which we all live could be a Matrix-style simulation, or even just a game on someone's computer. When scientists run simulations in our—apparently real—universe, they often simplify some of the physics, treating some things as constant, to help save processing power. However, in the universe we live in, physics has lots of apparently arbitrary constants, such as the speed of light in a vacuum. That's not reassuring.

The technologist Elon Musk—the man behind Tesla and Hyperloop—believes the simulated universe theory is correct, and given that there are likely millions or billions more simulated universes than real ones, statistics suggest we're probably not in a "base reality." Whether this leads you to decide, as the authors of this study did, that "nothing really matters" is more complicated. If our existence can only be said to exist through our perception of it, then this is still as meaningful as any other explanation for consciousness. As to the stability of our possibly simulated universe, science has yet to determine how likely it is that someone might kick out the power cable.

ARE YOU CALLING ME "DARLING"?

THE TING TINGS

In her lamentation on being regularly addressed by the wrong name, the Ting Tings' singer menacingly asks an unknown interlocutor whether he—we assume it's a he—is referring to her as "darling."

We do not have enough evidence to rule on whether he was or not—but we do have good evidence to suggest that unless he knows her well, he should not be doing so. The polling organization YouGov asked 4,191 adults whether or not it was acceptable for a man to call a woman he doesn't know well "darling," and only 11 percent responded that they thought it was—with men and women both agreeing the word was unacceptable. "Babe" scored slightly lower, at 7 percent, while "love" did better, with 25 percent thinking that was acceptable.

However, the Ting Tings may also wish to ponder why their names are forgotten. Experts offer reams of psychological explanations: when learning new names we're often also socially anxious; names get lost in our short-term memory, and names are just hard to remember—they're totally arbitrary collections of syllables, after all.

However, we can note one specific issue in this instance: in a five-minute thesis about name recollection, at no point does the Ting Tings' singer mention her name. For the record, it's Katie.

**TO FUEL THE THAMES FOR ONE SECOND,
THE PORTION OF THE GLOBAL POPULATION
WHO WOULD NEED TO CRY A TEAR**

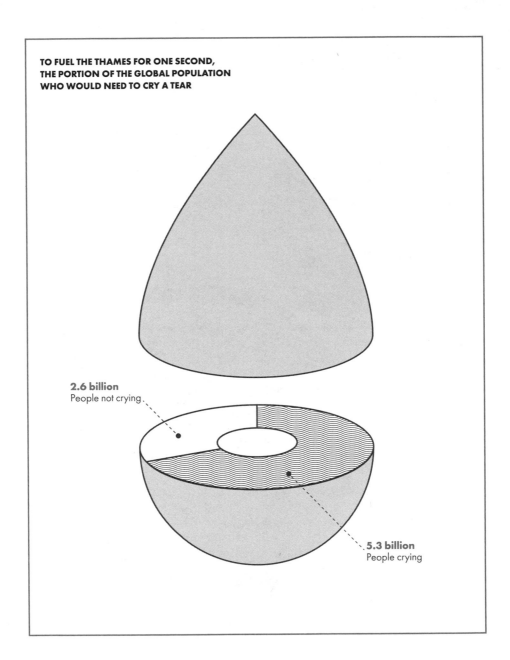

2.6 billion
People not crying

5.3 billion
People crying

HOW MUCH WOULD IT TAKE TO CRY A RIVER?

VARIOUS ARTISTS

For more than sixty years, people have issued public decrees to their former lovers to cry them a river, and claiming that they have done the same.

These range from London, J., to Bassey, S., to Streisand, B., to Timberlake, J. This story has been allowed to go unchallenged, and it shouldn't have: distressingly, the singers of these songs may not be telling the truth.

Rivers move a lot of water. The Amazon discharges 55 million gallons of water every single second. The rather more sluggish and far smaller Thames River in London discharges around 17,000 gallons each second. So, how many tears would we need to try to match the slower river? Research published in 1966 showed the average tear is 6.2 microliters in volume, suggesting that for a single gallon we need around 683,000 tears.

However, not many of us could manage much more than one tear per eye, no matter how hard we're trying. This means that to achieve even one second of discharge from a river as sluggish as the Thames, you'd need more than 5.3 billion people sobbing away. And given that to create a river people would have to keep up this output for quite some time, things are not looking good for Timberlake et al. Not only are they making deeply implausible claims to their former lovers, they're being somewhat overdemanding. Perhaps their breakups were for the best?

WHERE HAVE ALL THE FLOWERS GONE?

PETER, PAUL, AND MARY

Despite being seen by some as a rumination on mortality and war, Yarrow, P., Stookey, P., and Travers, M.'s, 1962 release, which builds on original research by Seeger, P., is in many ways a reflection on the economics of the global flower trade—which does indeed see thousands of tons of flowers traverse the globe every year.

These days, the place most of the flowers are leaving is the Netherlands, which is where almost half the flowers sold globally originate, followed by Colombia, Kenya, and Ecuador. But as to the trio's core question—where have they gone?—the answers lie close to home: the United States imports more than 80 percent of the flowers sold there, and in the UK that figure rises as high as 98 percent. Given that Yarrow, P., Stookey, P., and Travers, M., are from the US, the flowers are heading in their direction, which suggests that perhaps they'd have been better placed asking where the flowers were coming from. Their concern, however, may have been premature rather than misplaced: a peer-reviewed international botanical study in 2010 found that 25 percent of existing flowering plant species in the world are at risk of extension. For example, 97 percent of wildflower meadows in the UK have disappeared in the last hundred years. The flowers may not have gone yet, but many of them are at substantial risk of doing so—Yarrow, Stookey, and Travers were simply ahead of the curve with their fears. However, the complex mix of environmental, sociological, and climatological factors behind this aren't really contained in their proposed answer that girls have picked every one.

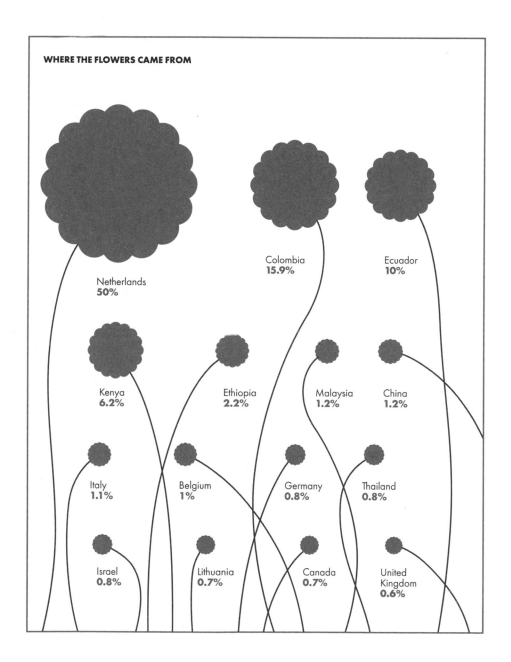

WHERE THE FLOWERS CAME FROM

Netherlands
50%

Colombia
15.9%

Ecuador
10%

Kenya
6.2%

Ethiopia
2.2%

Malaysia
1.2%

China
1.2%

Italy
1.1%

Belgium
1%

Germany
0.8%

Thailand
0.8%

Israel
0.8%

Lithuania
0.7%

Canada
0.7%

United
Kingdom
0.6%

TROUBLE RESULTING FROM STAYING VS. GOING

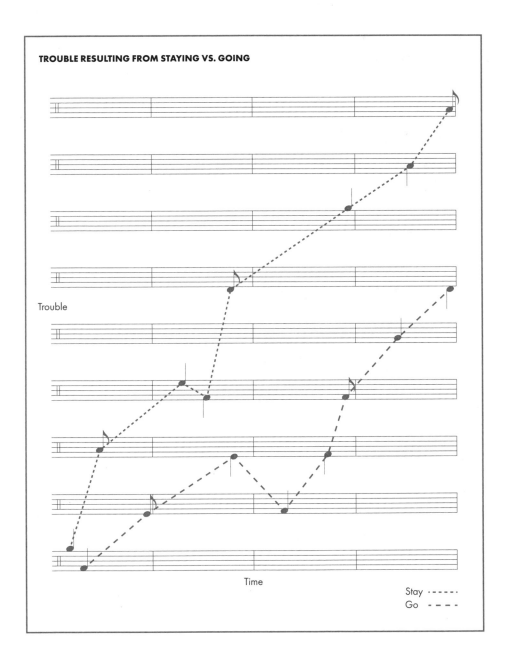

SHOULD I STAY OR SHOULD I GO?

THE CLASH

The problem presented by Jones, M., and his associates in the Clash is a dilemma over the best way to avoid a difficult situation, or "trouble."

The Clash has done well at identifying two courses of action—staying or going—and has reflected on the level of trouble each would cause, but repeatedly fails to decide on either over the three minutes ten seconds they allow themselves to make a decision.

Thankfully, a simple mathematical model helps us solve the trouble they're facing. Setting out their issue, the Clash states that there will be trouble if they go, but if they stay it will occur at twice that rate.

Defining trouble as t, we know that for any given value of trouble: $t(\text{go}) = x$, but $t(\text{stay}) = 2x$.

After this, it's simple math to say that for any level of trouble above zero—in which situation the Clash could do whatever they liked—they should clearly go, for a maximum of half as much trouble versus the alternative. We have also demonstrated that paying attention to algebra in school can prove useful in adult life after all.

However, we should stress the above analysis is all done under the hypothesis that Mr. Jones et al. wish to minimize the trouble they face, which may not be the case. They are, after all, named the Clash.

$$t(\text{go}) = x$$

but

$$t(\text{stay}) = 2x$$

DOES YOUR MOTHER KNOW THAT YOU'RE OUT?

ABBA

Everyone has had a moment during an evening out when things suddenly escalate quickly, whether into a potential bar fight, a blazing row, or just some quite maudlin talk.

But ABBA certainly takes no prisoners with their conversational gambits, rapidly switching from lightly flirting and dancing with the person their remarks are addressed to, to then asking them whether their mom knows that they're openly gay.

You might hope a band with such a significant LGBTQ following would know not to broach this topic so lightly, but this may be a consequence of the band's experiences among the often more liberal attitudes pervasive in Sweden. Then again, it's possible they are aware of significantly improving attitudes toward LGBTQ equality and are looking for confirmation that young people are benefiting from those trends. In 1982, three years after this song was released, only 45 percent of Americans said same-sex relations between consenting adults should be legal. By 2018, that figure had risen to 75 percent.

Survey evidence from the LGBTQ rights group Stonewall suggests ABBA may have been onto something with their question. People in their sixties said they had come out at an average age of thirty, while people in their thirties said they came out around twenty-one—but under-twenty-fives who had come out said they'd done so at an average age of seventeen. Turns out their mothers knew after all.

Of course, it's also possible ABBA was simply asking the teenager with whom they were dancing whether their parents were aware they were outside the house. That theory seems a little unlikely to the authors, though.

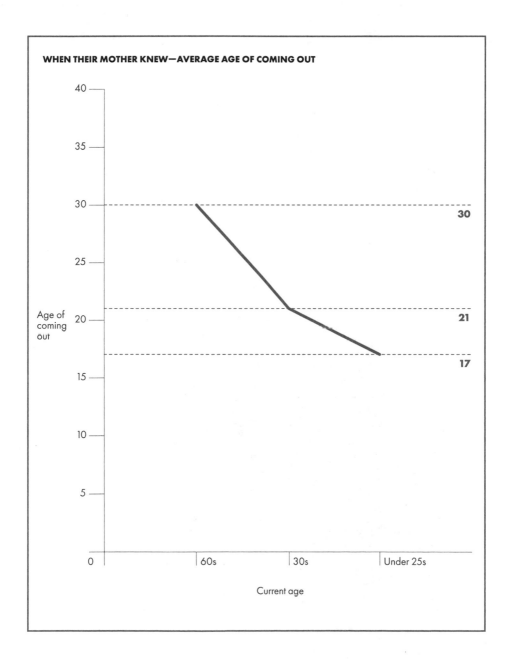

WHEN THEIR MOTHER KNEW—AVERAGE AGE OF COMING OUT

Age of coming out

30

21

17

0   60s   30s   Under 25s

Current age

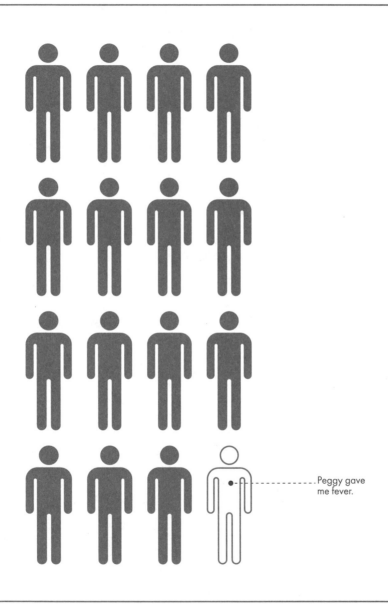

Peggy gave
me fever.

DO YOU GIVE ME FEVER?

PEGGY LEE

Lee, P., made her definitive contribution to this ongoing public health investigation in 1958, popularizing warnings against the dangers of contracting a fever from kissing, touching, and being held tight.

However, it appears that Lee's public health message wasn't backed up with especially strong evidence—certainly if she was referring to some of the more common ways in which fever is spread, such as the common cold.

As a key example, Lee is unlikely to get a fever through the common cold when she is kissed. Research conducted at the University of Wisconsin found that if someone with a cold infection kissed a number of other healthy volunteers for up to ninety seconds, just one in sixteen caught the infection. When it comes to this, no one is likely to give Lee fever.

Lee's other examples are much likelier to give her fever, though. If someone with a cold is holding her—tight or otherwise—they have a significantly higher chance of passing on their illness than through kissing, thanks to proximity to infected droplets in their breath. Lee's also right to spot that staying through the night is especially risky: eight hours sleeping with the possibility of coughs and splutters in close proximity to your face really might give you fever.

Lee's reputation as a public health expert comes out of the analysis pretty intact, with a small modification: you give me fever when you stay through the night, but not with a kiss.*

*Later studies into a fever specifically transmitted by dancing on a Saturday night by a "sweet city woman," or patient X as she became known, were found to be largely inconclusive.

WHAT WOULDN'T MEAT LOAF DO?

MEAT LOAF

Loaf, M.'s, extended profession of love has raised questions throughout the two decades since its release: scholars have asked time and again exactly what it is he is pledging that he would not do.

This is puzzling: Loaf is actually extremely specific in his treatise on what he would or would not do for love, specifically pledging just two things he would not do to his unnamed lover—he pledges never to lie to her, and never to screw around.

However, we should question whether Loaf's claim for unfailing honesty in this extended pledge stands up to scrutiny. Loaf variously claims in his song that the woman he loves sometimes "breathes fire" and is sometimes "carved in ice"—both claims that would revolutionize medical science if supported, as it is certainly unlikely that such extremes of temperature could be produced by one organism.

Loaf also claims he would run to hell and back—perhaps unaware that the strongest evidence for the physical existence of hell was a microphone supposedly lowered into Russia's Kola Superdeep borehole, which supposedly picked up screams of the anguished dead. Loaf may be unaware the story was eventually exposed as a hoax. Either way, it's not possible to run in a vertical borehole.

Finally, we must examine Loaf's claims to love his partner as long as planets are turning, stars burning, and other similar hyperboles extending into the billions of years. While Mr. Loaf managed twenty-five years of marriage before divorce—an admirable feat—this falls far short of his stated targets.

Reluctantly, we are forced to conclude that Loaf may in fact, on occasion, do just that.

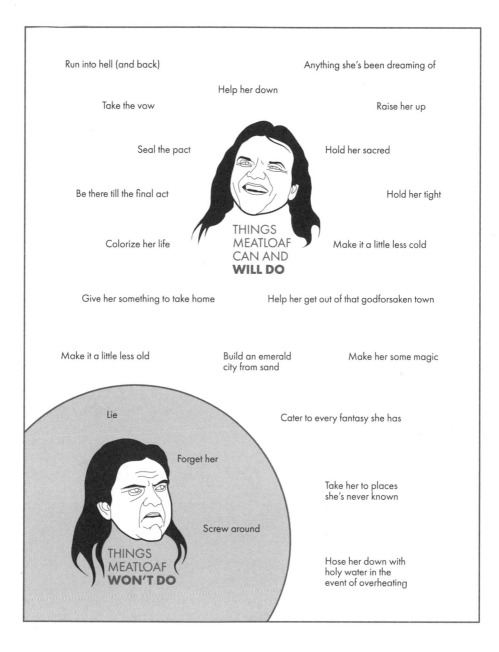

NOT VERY ELECTRIC: HOW MANY FRIENDS YOU NEED TO CHARGE YOUR PHONE

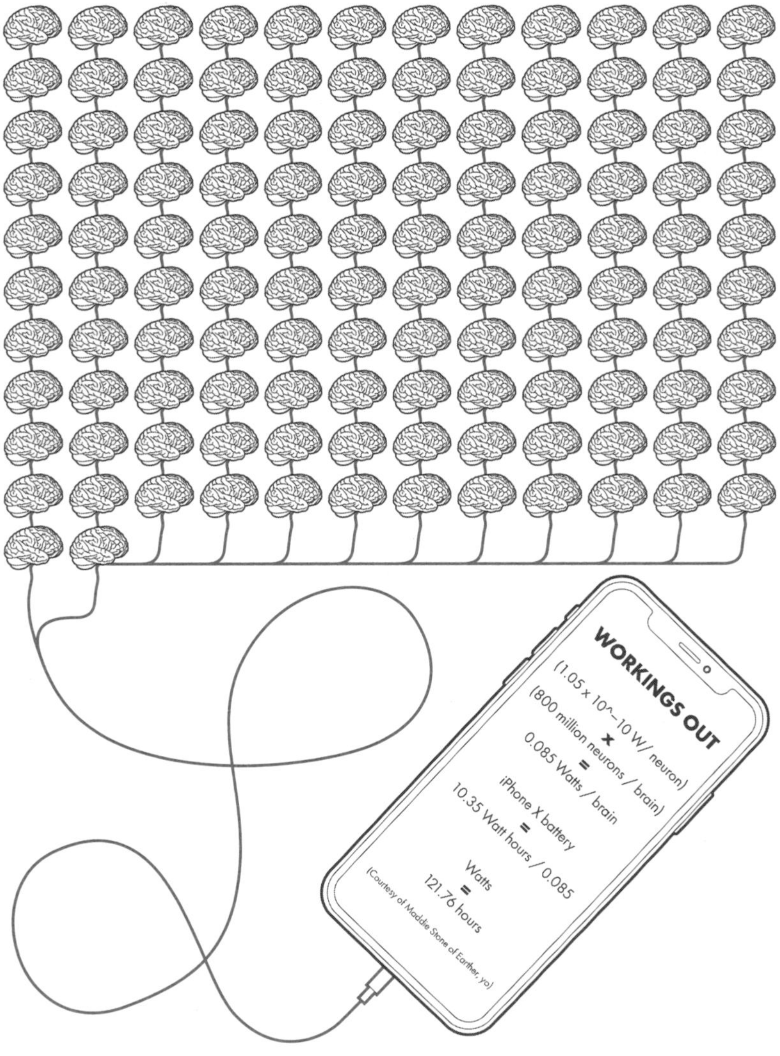

WORKINGS OUT

(1.05 x 10^-10 W / neuron)
x
(800 million neurons / brain)
=
0.085 Watts / brain

iPhone X battery
=
10.35 Watt hours / 0.085

Watts
=
121.76 hours

(Courtesy of Maddie Stone of Earther, yo)

ARE FRIENDS ELECTRIC?

GARY NUMAN

While experiencing difficulties with a "friend"—he describes how his friend appears to have "broke down"—Numan, G., wonders whether friends might be electric, a question fairly easily addressed by biological science.

Many of us will have experienced uncomfortable electric shocks when in the proximity of our friends, but these are typically the result of static electricity, caused by friction against certain types of clothing and other materials. While this is undoubtedly "electric" (and painful), it is more a result of our friends' sartorial choices than our friends themselves.

However, assuming that our friends are human—though much of this would hold for any live animal—they are at least capable of generating electricity, even if they cannot be said to be electric themselves. Neurologists have detected that each neuron inside a human brain is capable of carrying a voltage of around 0.07 volts.*

This voltage appears small—it's only 1/20th the voltage of a AA battery—but may be more impressive than it first appears. For one, a typical human has around 80 billion neurons in their brain, and for another, neurons are far smaller than AA batteries. Neurons carry their 0.07 volts across a tiny distance of just 0.000000005 meters, meaning that meter-for-meter they hold more than four times the electrostatic force involved in producing thunderstorms.

Human friends, therefore, are considerably electric—and if Numan's are not, he should perhaps seek urgent medical assistance for them.

---

*Other scholars have ventured it is instead "all about chemistry," a conjecture supported by the basis that merely to stay alive, each of the human body's 37 trillion cells needs to carry out at least 10 million chemical reactions per second. This is, in formal terms, a lot each day.

HOW DO YOU SOLVE A PROBLEM LIKE MARIA?

THE SOUND OF MUSIC

The nuns of Nonnberg Abbey appear to have a long list of problems with Maria, who is studying there to become a nun.

Maria, they complain, climbs trees and tears her clothes, whistles, dances, wears curlers, runs late, doesn't listen, and behaves unpredictably. These concerns—many of which may seem quite petty to a modern audience—are enough to make the group conclude that she is detrimental to the affairs of the abbey.

To look at how the issues with Maria could be addressed in the present day, the nuns could turn to feminist campaigner Caroline Criado Perez—but she firmly concludes that the problem does not lie where the nuns believe it does.

"Maria isn't the f---ing problem here," she argues. "The problem is a sexist society that has constructed a world around male bodies and male needs—and that then has

the gall to blame women for not fitting into it as expected. "Maria is a perfectly well-adjusted human being who just wants to be free to live according to her own rules and spin around in mountains singing at the top of her lungs; she doesn't care for your misogynistic expectations that she quietly acquiesces to being a member of the subordinate sex class. And if that's wrong, then I don't want to be right."

How do you solve a problem like Maria? You adjust your institutional expectations to properly accommodate her. A simple answer might be a more precise job description, allied with a rigorous appraisal structure and regular contact with a line manager. As with many questions, the answer is "better HR."

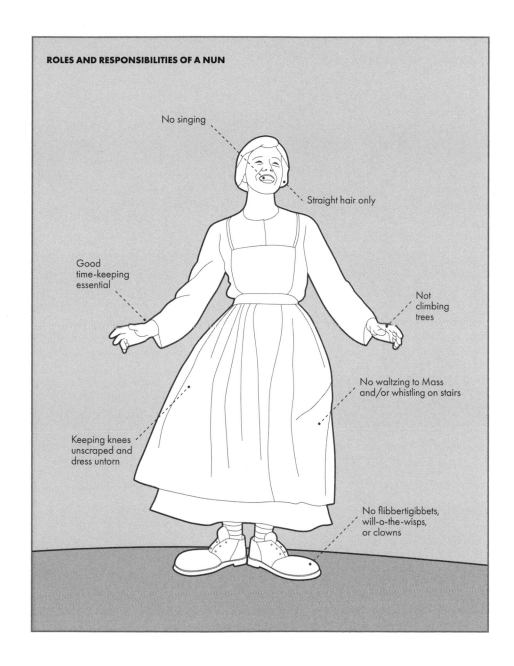

No singing

Straight hair only

Good time-keeping essential

Not climbing trees

No waltzing to Mass and/or whistling on stairs

Keeping knees unscraped and dress untorn

No flibbertigibbets, will-o-the-wisps, or clowns

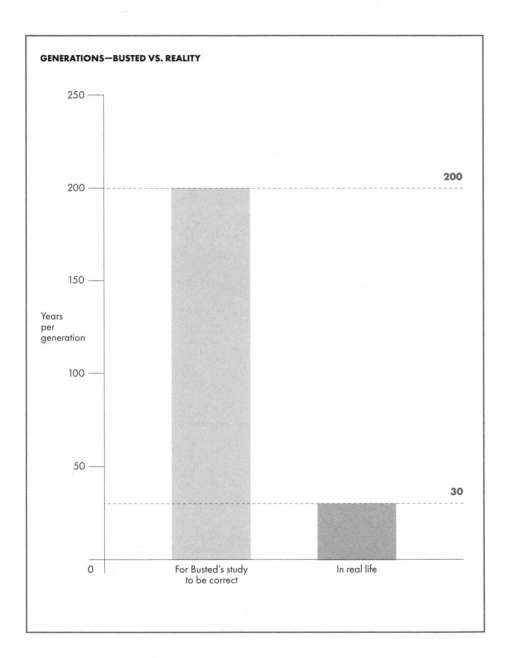

GENERATIONS—BUSTED VS. REALITY

Years per generation

250

200 · **200**

150

100

50

· **30**

0

For Busted's study to be correct   In real life

HOW MANY GENERATIONS WILL HAVE PASSED BY THE YEAR 3000?

BUSTED

In their oddly taunting 2002 account of their time-traveling experience, Busted is told that their "great-great-great-granddaughter" is "pretty fine"—information that is undoubtedly less useful to them than blueprints for advanced technologies, medicine, or even the results of events that can be gambled upon.

Nonetheless, the exchange raises an interesting question: at present, the average age for a woman to have her first child in most Western countries is in her mid-to-late twenties. Assuming this pattern held, we would expect Peter to encounter Busted's* great-(repeated 33 times) granddaughter, come the year 3000.

To suggest that they have instead met their companion's great-great-great granddaughter and found her not only alive but also conforming to 2002's standards of attractiveness suggests that perhaps the average generational span rapidly grew from around 30 years as it stands now to around 200 years. Even the most optimistic predictions for increased life span currently stand at 125 years over the next 50 years, with some researchers arguing that it will plateau at 115 years. Another solution could be that the final of the five generations attained infinite longevity, perhaps by downloading their consciousness into a powerful computer. In a future in which this is possible, perhaps that would be viewed as "pretty fine."

*The text is unclear as to whether the four members of Busted have collectively produced great-grandchildren through intermarriage in intervening generations, or whether "Peter"—their interlocutor—jumped to genealogical conclusions.

WHEN WILL I BE FAMOUS?

BROS

In the title of this study, Goss, L., and Goss, M., directly pose a complex statistical question—When can a typical person expect to become famous?—but it is one that they immediately give up any hope of answering.

Indeed, initially we are obliged to challenge the fundamental premise of their question—in the world as it stands, despite there being hundreds of TV channels and thousands of reality shows, it is still possible, even probable, that many people will never become famous.

If we look at data from imdb, an online repository of almost every film and TV show ever made, the site lists around 8.7 million people—but of those around two-thirds work behind the scenes, and so largely cannot be said to be famous. The Gosses specify that it's the sort of fame that results in their picture in the paper that they are interested in, and it is extremely unlikely that anyone but the most famous director or producer would be pictured in a newspaper. Neither would extras and actors in nonspeaking roles.

Even using a generous definition of fame that includes anyone credited for any speaking part in any show ever, still only 0.04 percent of us (or one in 2,500) will ever become famous.

Bros, however, treat fame as a certainty; it is after all "When will I?" not simply "Will I?," which possibly refers to Andy Warhol's assertion that everyone will be famous for fifteen minutes.

However, this gets difficult: if everyone is to be famous for fifteen minutes, we would need 199,771 years just to get through everyone alive right now. Or, to allow each person on the planet their allotted fifteen minutes in their lifetime, each person would have to share their fifteen minutes of fame with 2,496 others. That may not make you feel all that famous.

For the members of Bros themselves, however, the answer to the question posed by their song is simpler. This was their breakthrough hit, eventually reaching number two in the UK charts. It was released on November 16, and first charted on November 28, and Bros first appeared on *Top of the Pops* on January 21, 1988. So the answer to the question posed by Goss and Goss specifically is between twelve and thirty-five days after release.

Not famous

Famous

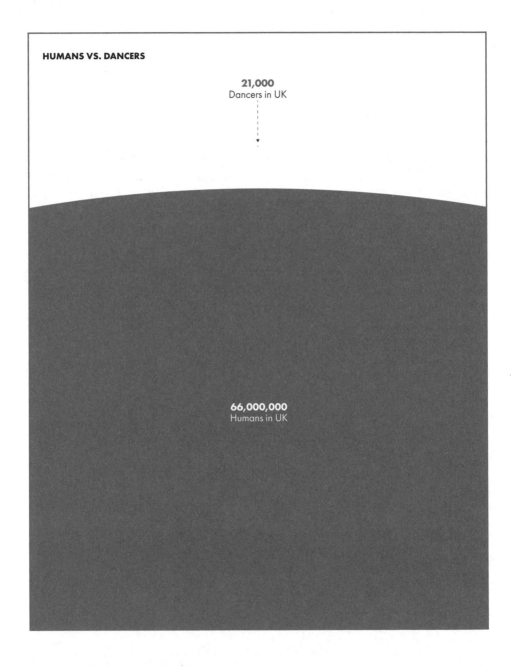

HUMANS VS. DANCERS

21,000
Dancers in UK

66,000,000
Humans in UK

ARE WE HUMAN, OR DANCER?

THE KILLERS

Flowers, B., urgently wants to know an answer to this question: he has sought it on his knees, and through the course of this thought experiment seems willing to cast aside many aspects of his life and character—including grace, virtue, soul, romance, and devotion—in his search.

It is unclear from the context how Flowers believes these aspects would have hindered him.

Leaving aside the implication in his question that dancers are somehow other than human, Flowers could have found an answer with far fewer sacrifices had he taken a more methodical approach to his research. Assuming that he means "dance professional," rather than simply someone who has ever danced in some way, which we can assume is close to everyone who has ever lived, then we can begin to build an answer.

In the UK, for example, Flowers could have examined data from the Office for National Statistics, and found 21,000 people are employed (or self-employed) as dancers and choreographers. Following that, we need only look up UK population estimates derived from the country's census to see that those 21,000 come from a population of around 66 million.

This lets us work out a possible solution to Flowers's question, if we accept his fundamental premise that the category dancer supersedes that of human: 99.97 percent of us should answer "human," but 0.03 percent are in the fortunate position of being able to answer "dancer" (or choreographer).

YOU WALK 500 MILES. YOU WALK 500 MORE. WHERE HAVE YOU BEEN?

THE PROCLAIMERS

The intended route of Reid, C. S., and Reid, C. M.'s, audacious 1,000-mile walk has been the subject of scholarly debate for the three decades since the release of their account.

Working from the assumption that the brothers are starting from their hometown of Leith—a suburb of Scotland's capital, Edinburgh—people have tried to calculate how far they would get if they walked "500 miles" and then "500 more."

In 2014, Hazel McKendrick made an estimate on Twitter that 500 miles would take the brothers as far as northern France, or northeastern Germany, while the promised additional 500 would allow them to reach Poland, Austria, or Italy. However, as South Carolina–based cartographer Kenneth Field noted, this took no notice of obstacles such as mountains or oceans, or even of the curvature of the Earth. Using estimates based on Europe's existing roads (though assuming the brothers could walk on water), he came up with more modest travel distances: 500 miles would only get them to two points of mainland Europe, while with 500 more they could begin to reach the south of France.

Even this more rigorous calculation, though, missed two important considerations. Firstly—unless they have covered up this fact superbly—the Proclaimers cannot walk on water. Secondly, during the course of their song, they say the purpose of their 1,000-mile walk would be to fall at the door of the person they're singing to. If we work on the assumption that door is also in Leith, the Proclaimers' wish can realistically come true: if they walk to Land's End in Cornwall—the furthest they can walk without hitting ocean—they will have traveled 545 miles. So if they want to end where they began, they can walk 500 miles, then 500 more, but then they would have to do an extra 90.2 miles before falling down right where they started, in Leith. If, however, they wanted to walk only 1,000 miles exactly, but still visit mainland Britain's most westerly point, they would be able to make it back up to the north of England to somewhere in the vicinity of the Currock area, just south of Carlisle.

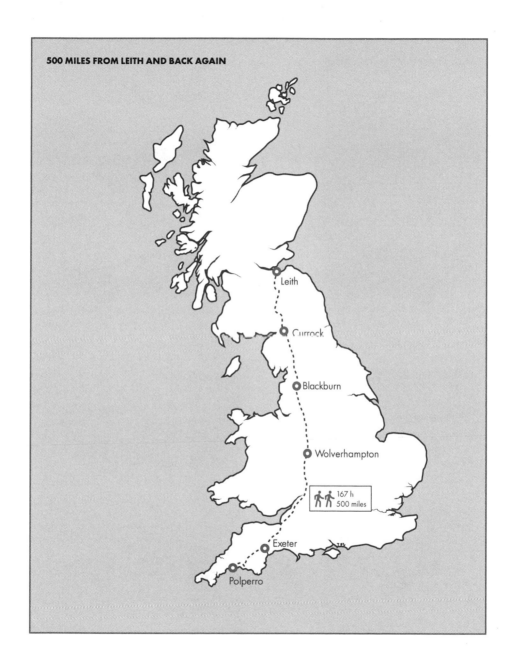

500 MILES FROM LEITH AND BACK AGAIN

Leith

Currock

Blackburn

Wolverhampton

167 h
500 miles

Exeter

Polperro

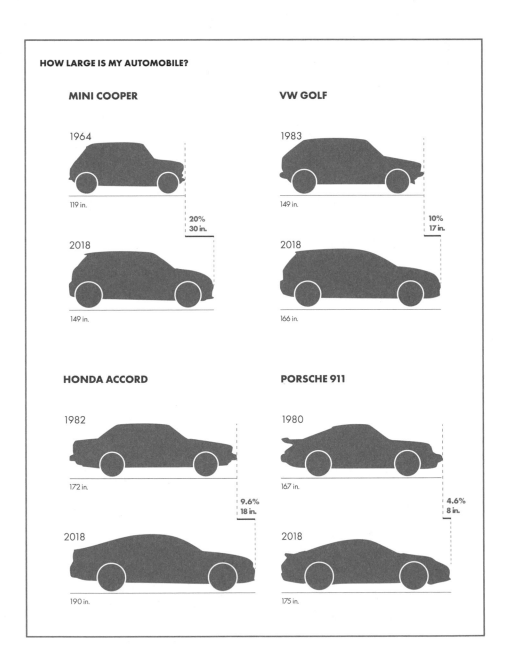

HOW LARGE IS MY AUTOMOBILE?

MINI COOPER

1964

119 in.

20%
30 in.

2018

149 in.

VW GOLF

1983

149 in.

10%
17 in.

2018

166 in.

HONDA ACCORD

1982

172 in.

9.6%
18 in.

2018

190 in.

PORSCHE 911

1980

167 in.

4.6%
8 in.

2018

175 in.

WHERE IS MY LARGE AUTOMOBILE?

TALKING HEADS

This is a song that has been characterized as being perhaps the ultimate musical rendition of a midlife crisis—and so concern about the size and presence of the family patriarch's car was an almost vital ingredient.

Repeated psychological studies have found happiness correlates not just with our own income and status, but with how we are doing compared to those around us. For example, a 2009 US-wide study found that people were happier when they lived in a rich neighborhood in a poor county than in a similarly rich neighborhood in a rich county—suggesting the issue for Talking Heads is not so much the size of their car, but whether or not it's bigger than other people's.

This is where time has acted against Talking Heads since they recorded the song in 1980: despite climate change and air pollution suggesting cars should get smaller, they have instead gotten bigger across the decades. Figures from automotive.com show a modern Porsche 991 is eight inches longer than a 1980 Porsche 911. A modern VW Golf is seventeen inches longer than a 1983 model; Honda Accords have grown eighteen inches since 1982, and a modern Mini Cooper is thirty inches longer than the original.

Herein lies a possible cause for Talking Heads' social anxiety: their automobile might have been large by 1980 standards, but now it's bound to seem small.

DID THOSE FEET IN ANCIENT TIMES WALK UPON ENGLAND'S MOUNTAINS GREEN?

WILLIAM BLAKE

In his rather confused 1804 investigation into a potential site for Jerusalem in a northern English location, Blake, W., sets out a number of questions that are easily answered and dismissed.

The song also includes a number of actions that would likely be impossible, or dangerous if attempted, warranting a full safety and fact-checking effort.

While there is a period of Jesus's life about which the Bible says nothing, all of Jesus's recorded activities occur within what is modern-day Israel—in Nazareth, Bethlehem, and Jerusalem—with no evidence he came to England. We now tackle Blake's other questions and issues in turn.

And was the holy Lamb of God / On England's pleasant pastures seen? / And did the countenance divine shine forth / Upon our clouded hills? Blake is fooling no one here: these are repetitions of his first question, to which the answer is still no.

And was Jerusalem builded here / Among those dark Satanic mills? No. Jerusalem is located in the Middle East and claimed by Israel and Palestine as their capital—it does not need England staking a claim, too. Additionally, it was established there since at least four centuries before Christ, whereas the "dark Satanic mills" did not appear until two millennia later.

Bring me my bow of burning gold. If you see a bow of burning gold, do not touch it: it will burn you.

Bring me my arrows of desire. Desire is intangible and therefore would not be suitable material for arrows.

Bring me my chariot of fire. Please see the warnings on the bow of burning gold.

Till we have built / In England's green and pleasant land. Jerusalem, as has been repeatedly stated, has already been built. And not in England. Whether or not Blake, W., was advocating a kind of biblical proto-theme park as a means of kick-starting the northern British tourist trade is unclear.

**JERUSALEM, UK—
BIBLICAL PROTO-THEME PARK**

Jerusalem, UK

TREES NEEDED TO SEQUESTER THE CARBON FOR VIDEO VIEWS, APPROXIMATELY THE SAME AS IN THE LONDON BOROUGH OF HARROW

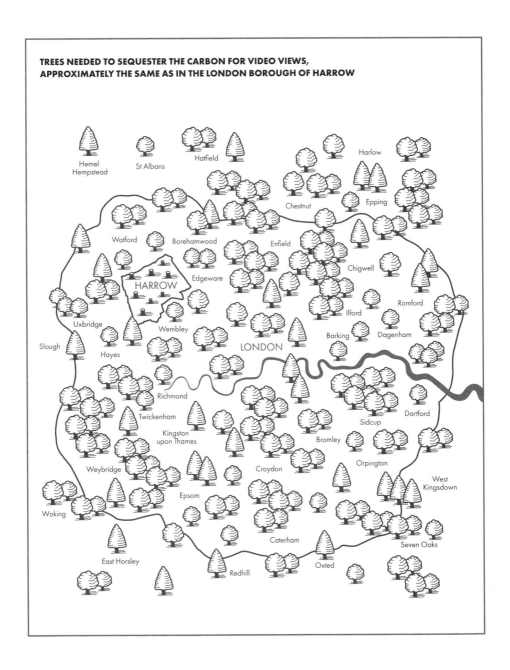

ARE WE OUT OF THE WOODS YET?

TAYLOR SWIFT

The question posed here by environmental scientist Swift, T., in her 2014 study is clearly one of deep concern to her, as she repeats it no fewer than thirty-eight times in her four-minute-sixteen-second video.

Yet it should come as no surprise that Swift regards it as so important, as the issue of deforestation is crucial to the future of the world. Not only can deforestation lead to mudslides and other localized catastrophes, but the absence of forests reduces the Earth's ability to absorb carbon dioxide, accelerating climate change. Swift is rightly drawing our attention to such things.

Fortunately, we are not entirely out of woods and forests yet, but we are running out of them rapidly. Around 10,000 years ago, according to UN data, the planet had 6 billion hectares of forest, covering around 45 percent of the Earth's land area. Today, that's down to around 4 billion hectares, or just 31 percent of the world's land.

It's also disappearing faster each year: over the last 5,000 years we've lost around 360,000 hectares of forest a year. In the current decade we lose more than 5 million hectares every year. We might not be out of the woods yet, but the situation is certainly not improving—so no wonder Swift is so worried.

Ironically though, we know that each 10-minute YouTube view produces 0.035 oz of carbon, so her four-minute-sixteen-second video produces 0.0146 oz. At the time of writing it has been viewed 145,623,180 times, producing 2,126,098 oz or 132,881 pounds of carbon. If a single tree can sequester 46.2 pounds of carbon a year, then we need 2,876 extra trees just to deal with the carbon generated from watching this video.

I WILL SURVIVE— BUT FOR HOW LONG?

GLORIA GAYNOR

Many people who have experienced a difficult breakup have been reassured by Gaynor, G.'s, classic investigation into stoicism to help get them through heartbreak.

Research suggests most of us experience our first serious breakup at around the age of 20—a little younger than Gaynor's age when she first posed this question. The US's official life expectancy tables reveal that, at that stage, while a man can expect to survive for another 57 years, a woman can expect another 61.6 years on Earth—meaning that statistically speaking, Gaynor will not only survive, but also outlive her former partner.

There is also reassurance for people separating from even more serious or long-standing relationships: the average age of a divorcing man is forty-six, meaning he should expect another thirty-three years alive to find another love. The news is better for women, who are on average aged forty-three when they divorce, meaning they can expect to survive a full forty years more.

However, returning to Gaynor's study, her assertion that she has "all her life to live" is less accurate. If we use the example of a woman who is 20 when she experiences her first breakup and lives to be 81.6, she has in fact only 75 percent of her life left to live at that point. However, Gaynor was first making this statement when she was 29 years old, meaning that she had around 64 percent of her life left to live, with every 18 months reducing that figure by another percentage point. As Gaynor, G., is now 69 years old, when she makes this statement she has only 15 percent of her life to live. We can represent this as a curve on a graph with age at which you sing the song against the percentage of remaining life left to live.

Gaynor's missive will certainly survive, however: in 2015 it was added to the USA's National Recording Registry, to be preserved for future generations.

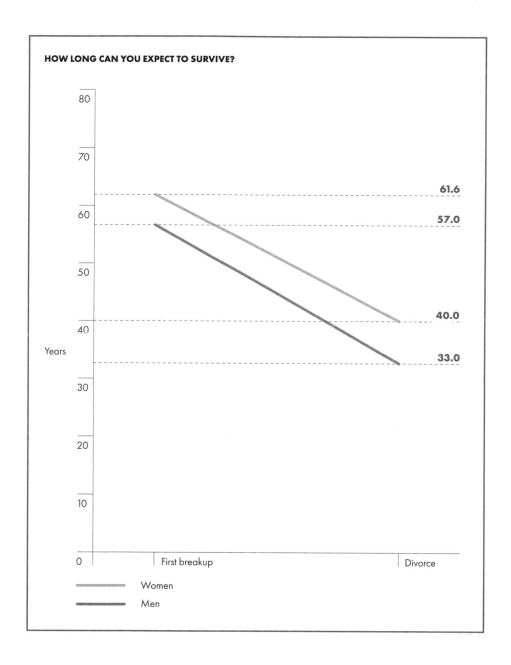

HOW LONG CAN YOU EXPECT TO SURVIVE?

Years

First breakup

Divorce

.... Women

———— Men

61.6

57.0

40.0

33.0

DIVORCED

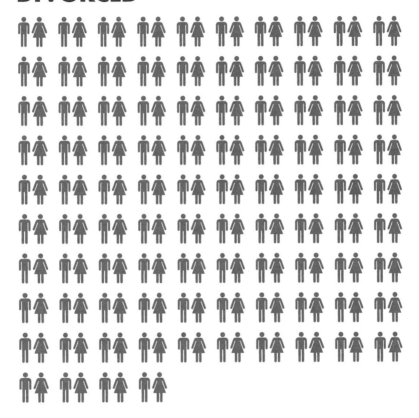

REMARRIED

Long-lasting happiness

IF YOU DON'T LOVE ME NOW, WILL YOU NEVER LOVE ME AGAIN?

FLEETWOOD MAC

If any people could claim to know in detail the complexities of love, betrayal, separation, and dealing with ex-lovers, then it would be the members of Fleetwood Mac—who have managed virtually every combination of marriage, cheating, and separation over their tumultuous history.

As such, their assertion that once the chain is broken—when you fall out of love—that will be the end forever would seem to be one that we would all do well to believe. However, it's not strictly true.

If we look at divorce, perhaps the most obvious and complete a split that a serious relationship can have, we can see evidence that sometimes you can break the chain. A study of 1,001 divorced couples published in 2005 by Dr. Nancy Kalish found that 6 percent of divorced couples eventually remarried their former spouse, and in the instances where they do, they have a much better than average chance of staying together, with 72 percent of the marriages lasting.

This may have been particularly on the minds of this study's authors at the time as both Buckingham, L., and Nicks, S., McVie, J., and C., and Fleetwood, M., were all in the process of ending their long-term relationships at the point at which it was published. It is perhaps a comfort that the high volume of failed relationships within the band actually increases the likelihood of one of them being rekindled.

More generally, Kalish found that the remarrying couples who fared best were those who married young and then waited several decades before reuniting—suggesting that if you do break the chain, it's best to wait a long time before trying to repair it.

HOW MUCH SPACE DO A MILLION PHOTOGRAPHS TAKE UP?

THE VAPORS

Fenton, D., famously raises this question in his problematic investigation of self-identity as it relates to race.

His thesis is that taking a lot of photos is "turning" him Japanese. Leaving aside this simplistic and problematic model of racial identity, the study does yield one important point.

Fenton refers to wanting a million pictures of his lover, which, when the study was first published in 1980, would have meant physically printed-out photos. Many people hear the lyric as Fenton wanting a million pictures on his "self"—meaning that if the photos were standard 6-inch by 4-inch size, he would need a surface area 7,936 times larger than the typical person. However, this is a misreading: Fenton is actually stating he wants a million photos in his "cell." To fit that many 6-inch by 4-inch photos, his cell would need to be 200 feet long, 200 feet wide, and 200 feet high—rather a lot bigger than the standard 6-foot by 9-foot US isolation cell.

In the modern era, things are simpler. A typical iPhone image is around one megabyte, meaning a million would be one million megabytes, or one terabyte—which can now be stored on a portable drive that's smaller and not much thicker than a 6-inch by 4-inch photograph.

That convenience is essential to some of the internet's biggest businesses: one million photographs—enough to line our 200-foot cell—are uploaded to Instagram every 15 minutes, 24 hours a day, making a total just short of 100 million each day, or 12 billion a year. It's likely a good thing for the world's trees that these don't get printed out anymore.

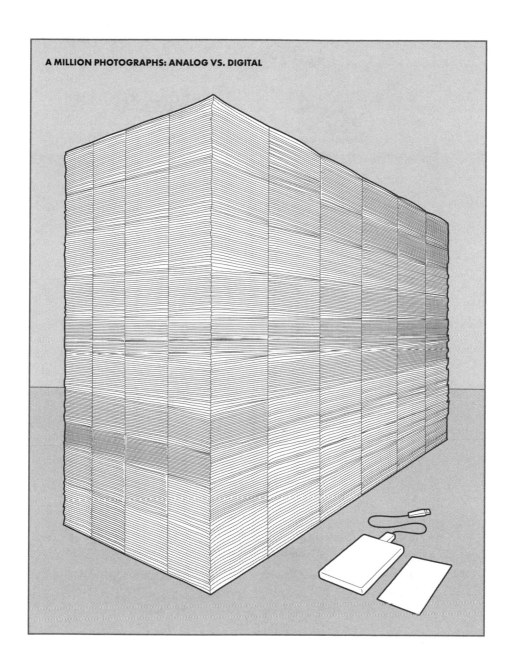

A MILLION PHOTOGRAPHS: ANALOG VS. DIGITAL

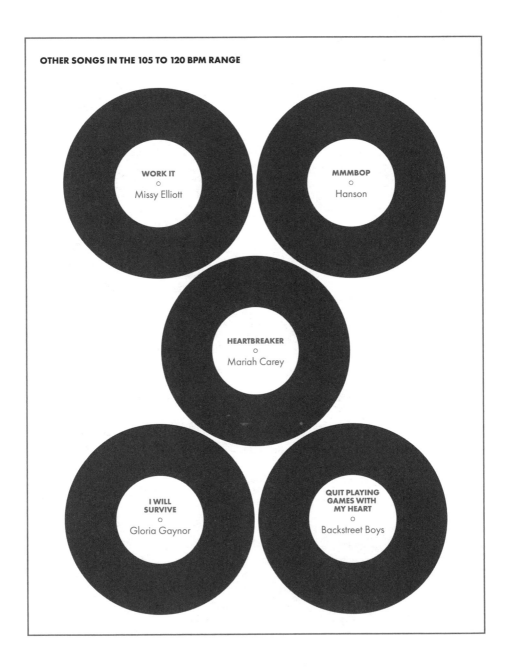

WORK IT
○
Missy Elliott

MMMBOP
○
Hanson

HEARTBREAKER
○
Mariah Carey

I WILL SURVIVE
○
Gloria Gaynor

QUIT PLAYING GAMES WITH MY HEART
○
Backstreet Boys

IS ANNIE OKAY?

MICHAEL JACKSON

Simply from the description that Jackson, M., gives in this case study, anyone should be able to determine that Annie is not entirely okay: we know there are bloodstains on the carpet, that she's been struck down and even that it was her doom—so the signs do not look good for Annie.

However, the story isn't quite what many of us might think it is. "Annie, are you okay?" was a key line taught when training people to perform CPR, as one of the most common models of CPR dummies was known as Resusci Anne, or Annie for short—an unusually realistic model of a dummy with a face based on the death mask of an unknown woman found drowned in the Seine in the late 1880s. So what Jackson, M., is setting out here is just a particularly elaborate scenario in CPR training.

However, if Annie is relying on CPR to survive, she is unlikely to be okay: the overall survival rate of people receiving CPR in a hospital is just 10.6 percent, and that falls still lower for those who need CPR outside.*

To give Annie the best chance of survival, the chest compressions should be administered to her as near to one hundred beats per minute as possible. One way to try to keep this beat is to have the song "Stayin' Alive" in mind, as it has a tempo of 103 bpm. Closer still, though, is the Queen song "Another One Bites the Dust"—though anyone administering CPR to this tune is strongly advised not to sing it out loud, for fear of giving the wrong impression to onlookers and the casualty.

---

*By contrast, survival rates can be as high as 90 percent for those who receive electric defibrillation within a minute of cardiac arrest, vindicating studies that talk about electricity in your veins.

HOW MANY HONEYS MAKE THEIR MONEY?

DESTINY'S CHILD

At multiple points during this socioeconomic rallying cry, Knowles, B., Rowland, K., and Williams, M., call on all the women who make their own money to throw up their hands—which naturally raises the question as to how many people in any given population would be eligible to wave their hands in response.

The proportion of women who work and so earn at least some income has increased dramatically in the last few generations: in 1971 just 53 percent of women in the UK were in any kind of employment (versus 92 percent of men), while in the most recent UK statistics that figure had jumped to an all-time high of 71 percent (versus 80 percent for men).

This would suggest almost three-quarters of women in the audience could throw their hands up. However, the song has a stronger suggestion: that these women are in a relationship, but are financially independent of their partner—but data suggests that a situation in which a woman exactly equals or outearns her husband is much rarer.

Research for the USA's National Bureau of Economic Research found that US couples were much less likely to match if the woman outearned the man, and that marriage rates declined in areas where women outearned men—meaning that for some reason richer women and poorer men do not generally want to marry. Worse still for high-earning women, marriages where the woman earned more were found to be less happy and more likely to end in divorce.

In most marriages, it seems, the man still serves as the main breadwinner. One notable exception, of course, is Beyoncé herself: despite her husband, Jay-Z, being richer overall, she outearns him by more than two dollars for each dollar he brings in: she netted $105 million in 2017 versus Jay-Z's measly $42 million.

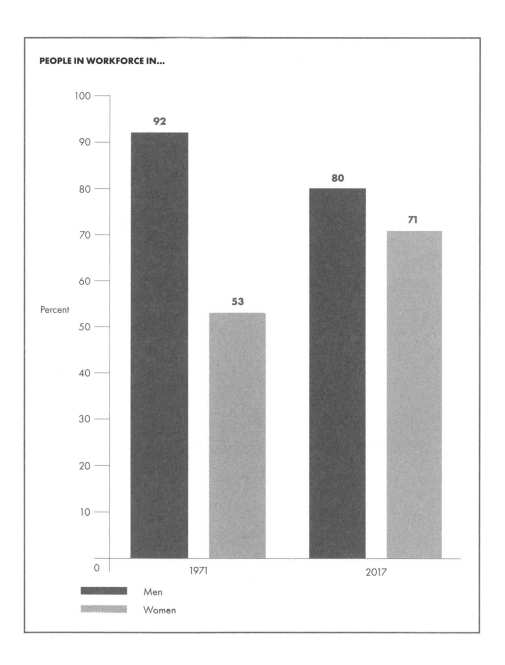

PEOPLE IN WORKFORCE IN...

Men
Women

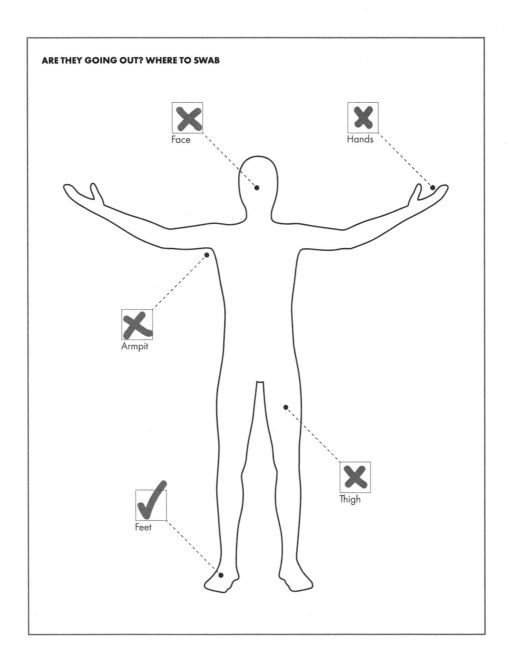

IS SHE REALLY GOING OUT WITH HIM?

JOE JACKSON

Jackson, J., is determined to know the relationship status of people around him in this famous 1979 study and seems unwilling to simply ask any of the people concerned whether or not they will be going home together.

Early in the song he even notes that he has heard that one of the women whose relationship he is questioning is married or engaged "or something"—but as the study predates online search engines and social media sites he was, of course, unable to use these resources to confirm the information. This study therefore offers us a nice opportunity to consider other ways of answering the central question.

Jackson could attempt to work out the relationships by looking for body language cues, such as hand-holding or kissing, or by watching for signs of what psychologists call "emotional contagion," as people begin to mirror the speech patterns of someone they spend a lot of time with. Or he could simply look to see whether or not the people concerned are wearing wedding rings, but he seems to be eager for a higher level of certainty than that.

Happily, modern science can help. A 2017 study published in the American Society for Microbiology's journal, *mSystems*, revealed that by analyzing the microbiome—the ecosystem of bacteria on people's skin, cohabiting couples can be identified by a computer algorithm (which had access to no other information) with 86 percent accuracy. The microbiome is affected by a number of factors around the home: such as whether the couple owns pets, what skin products they use, alcohol consumption, and more.

The most useful skin swabs for matches are those taken from the soles of the feet. So for Jackson to get a relatively reliable answer to his question, he need only obtain foot swabs from the couples concerned—surely a simple undertaking, if he is as interested as he professes to be.

WILL THIS BE THE DAY THAT YOU DIE?

DON MCLEAN

In his tribute to Buddy Holly, McLean, D., quotes men singing this will be the day they die.

Calculating the chances that they are right is a complex task: it depends on our sex, our age, our health, and what country we're in.

The chance of dying in any given year changes dramatically over the course of our lifetime: at the age of 20 we have around a one in 1,000 chance of dying that year, whereas by 80 those odds have risen to a much more worrying one in 10. However, the men were being far more specific than that—they're claiming they'll die today. Working that out gets far trickier, as it hugely depends on what you're doing on that day: a day in bed will be much less risky than a day motorbiking to your job down a coal mine.

Statistics experts David Spiegelhalter and Michael Blastland came up with a novel way of measuring this risk—the "micromort," a measure for a one-in-a-million chance of death. Taking a single ecstasy pill is roughly one micromort, as there is a one-in-a-million chance of it killing you. Heroin, by contrast, would be 377 micromorts. Traveling a mile on a motorbike is one micromort, the same as 7,500 miles by commercial flight.

We know that the three old men were drinking "whiskey and rye," presumably near the dry levee. The fact they were singing would suggest they had been drinking for a while. The micromort calculations of drinking by a river are not available, but we do know that each double whiskey the ole boys knocked back would reduce their life expectancy by around 9 minutes.

But what are the bigger risks that would significantly increase the chances of this being the day you die? One huge risk is childbirth—at 2,100 micromorts—but the highest risk Spiegelhalter and Blastland mention is flying on a bombing raid during the Second World War: 25,000 micromorts per trip, easily enough to give the song sung by "the good ole boys" an unnerving chance of being correct.

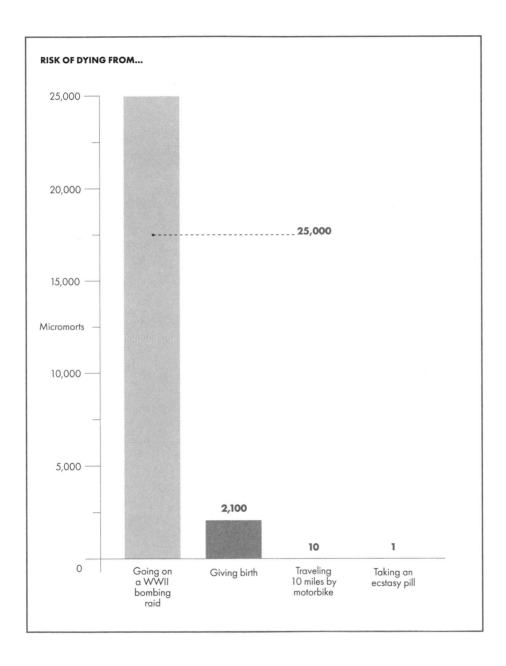

RISK OF DYING FROM...

25,000 ┄┄┄┄┄┄┄┄┄┄┄┄┄┄ **25,000**

2,100

10   **1**

Going on a WWII bombing raid

Giving birth

Traveling 10 miles by motorbike

Taking an ecstasy pill

Micromorts

CAN YOU FEEL THE LOVE TONIGHT?

ELTON JOHN AND TIM RICE

Most humans would struggle to articulate any specific way they could feel love among the population in general on any given night: unlike many species, we do not have a specific mating season, and our conscious brains can't detect love in other people—we may pick up on signs of it, but we are only really aware of it when we feel it ourselves.

However, it can easily be argued that in this study, John, E., and Rice, T., are talking about lions, and in this case there is an argument that big cats are capable of feeling love in the air. The reason comes down to pheromones.*

To mark territory, lions and other big cats spray urine that contains more and different pheromones than regular urine. That mix changes over time, and includes signals as to whether or not the animal is looking to reproduce. Thanks to some clever quirks of biology that make the scents linger for a long time, potential sexual partners can feel the love in the air not just for a night but for much longer periods than that. This is what the study's other contributors, Messrs. Timon and Pumbaa, may be referring to as the "romantic atmosphere" and the "disaster" in the air.

This can work against the animals concerned, though. It was observed as early as the nineteenth century that the sensitive antennae of moths are capable of detecting the chemicals emitted by a would-be mate from a great distance. That is now turned against them: when farmers want to rid themselves of moths as a pest, they release female pheromones to attract them by the thousands to traps. Animals may be able to feel love in the air—but it opens them up to industrial-scale honey traps.

---

*Whether or not an equivalent of signaling pheromones for humans even exists is a topic of much debate. Recent studies suggest that two of the most likely "putative human pheromones"—androstadienone and estratetraenol—should be dropped.

CALL ME, MAYBE?

CARLY RAE JEPSEN

At first glance it is difficult to see why Jepsen, C. R., believes what she's asking is in any way "crazy": she has met someone she's attracted to, passed over her number, and invited him to call her—a routine event on nights out for decades.

Indeed, it is tempting to see this—along with Jepsen's use of the classical rhetorical technique *sprezzatura*, in which a studied nonchalance is used to mask your true feelings, with her addition of "maybe"—as an attempt to muddy the waters of how much this exchange means to her.

It's only when we start to think about the phone-use habits of millennials that we understand why what Jepsen is doing seems crazy to her: she is inviting a call from someone she doesn't know, whereas most millennials would expect a text, or a WhatsApp message.

Official research by Ofcom, the UK's phone regulator, shows that only 15 percent of 16- to 24-year-olds consider phone calls the most important form of communication, versus 36 percent who think instant messaging takes the top spot and making phone calls is something of a niche form of communication.

Indeed, there's a surge of people who barely use their phone as a phone at all. A study by Ipsos MORI found that in 2012 in the UK just 4 percent of people who owned a mobile phone made less than one phone call a week from it. Within just three years this had climbed to 25 percent.

MESSAGE ME, MAYBE?

36%

15%

Instant messaging   Phone calls

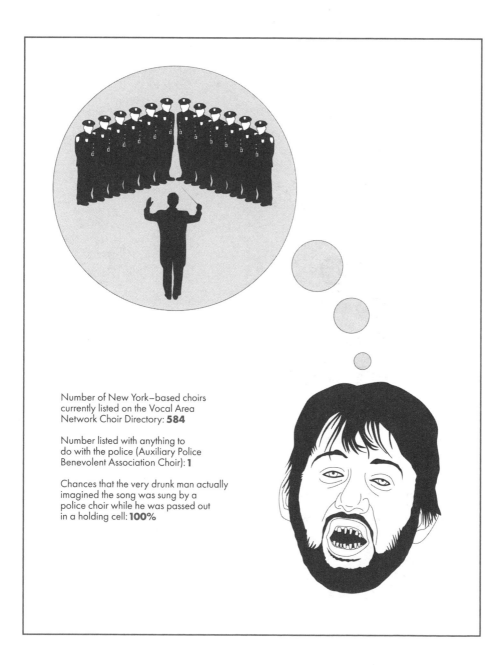

Number of New York–based choirs currently listed on the Vocal Area Network Choir Directory: **584**

Number listed with anything to do with the police (Auxiliary Police Benevolent Association Choir): **1**

Chances that the very drunk man actually imagined the song was sung by a police choir while he was passed out in a holding cell: **100%**

WERE THE BOYS OF THE NYPD CHOIR SINGING "GALWAY BAY"?

THE POGUES

Since its creation in 1988, this exploration of the role of institutional vocal groups in New York has become a benchmark for our understanding of Christmas.

It describes a man singing from the drunk tank—a police lockup for people too drunk to remain unarrested—to a lover he's dragged down to his level, about a time when things were better for the two of them.

The singer recollects the music playing as the two of them met—the song "Galway Bay," about the scenic bay on the west coast of Ireland. There are two versions of the song, one popular in the bay itself (oddly, this version is the only one to mention an American state), and one popular in the USA.

The song was, according to the song's narrator, being sung by the men of the NYPD's choir—which would seem logical, given the historical connections between New York's Irish community and its police force. However, the NYPD did not in 1987, when the song was released, and does not in the present day have a voice choir. The nearest it comes is a collection of pipers and drummers, who play as part of its Emerald Society (and who feature in the music video).

Given the singer's inebriated status, it would be unsurprising if he had misremembered a detail of when he met the love of his life, but as the two of them are unlikely to share the same false memory of a song, it raises an unanswerable question: Who was singing "Galway Bay"?

IS MONEY THE ROOT OF ALL EVIL TODAY?

PINK FLOYD

In their assessment of the state of the capitalist global economy, Waters, R., Gilmour, D., et al., debate whether it can be accurately stated that money—presumably in the form of fiat currency—is the source of societal ills.

Waters carefully caveats his assertion in his thesis, appending the allegation against money with "so they say," a frustratingly vague manner of attribution. It is possible Waters has been misled into inaccurately citing the Bible, which notes that "love of money," not money itself, is the root of evil.

Empirically, we can assess that if Waters et al. regard substantial wealth inequality as an "evil," then they will find themselves with a strong evidence basis to support their claims. Research published in January 2018 by Oxfam found that the world's richest 42 people owned as much wealth as its poorest 3.7 billion, and that the global top 1 percent have 82 percent of the world's wealth.

Defenders of the capitalist system, and of money, could note that barter economies have huge inefficiencies and transaction costs—if you're trying to swap a tool for food, you may need to do numerous trades to get there. They may also note that between 1987 and 2013 the number of people living in extreme poverty across the globe dropped from 35 percent to less than 11 percent.

Waters et al. may be more concerned with the other end of the distribution, though. In their discourse, they note with regret that while they are in the "high-fidelity first-class traveling set," they feel they need—but lack—a Learjet.

Top 1%

Rest of
the world

TIME UNTIL YOU'D GET RUN OVER DOING IT...

RURAL ROAD DEATH

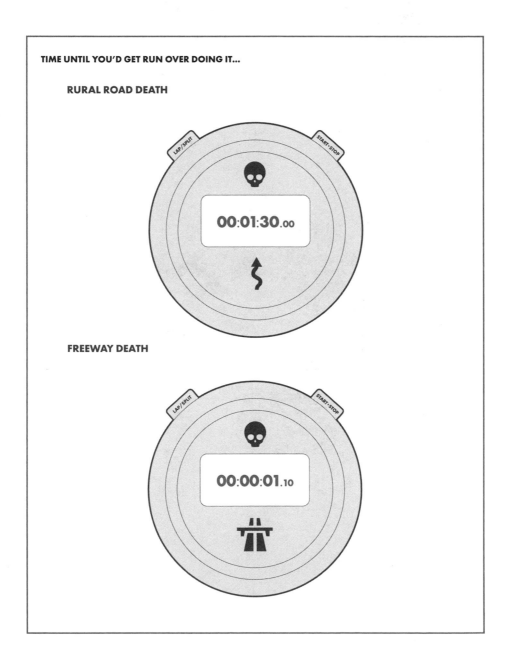

FREEWAY DEATH

WHY DON'T WE DO IT IN THE ROAD?

THE BEATLES

Lennon, J., and McCartney, P., receive near-universal acclaim as two of the greatest thinkers in human history, and so this study's simplicity—13 of its 16 lines are simply a repetition of its titular question—can only be explained by assuming that one or both men really, really wanted to have sex in the road.

The obvious answer to this question would simply be a fear of getting hit by a vehicle, something that would surely put a dampener on even the best intercourse. Data lets us work out whether or not that fear is well founded: a 2017 survey shows the average UK adult says a sex session lasts for nineteen minutes—ten minutes of foreplay, and nine minutes of intercourse. We will assume that in the interests of road safety that couples in this case would be willing to forgo the foreplay.

The chances of surviving a nine-minute sex session in a road will naturally depend on the type of road. Statistics from the UK Department of Transport allow us to work this out in detail. The Beatles should definitely rule out freeways—the typical stretch of freeway sees 81,000 cars pass every twenty-four hours, meaning a car would pass every 1.1 seconds. This would suggest a couple could expect to be run over nearly 540 times in a typical session.

The safest option—and one that tallies with Lennon and McCartney's promise that no one would see the couple doing it— would be to use a minor rural road, which is the least likely to be overlooked and the quietest in traffic terms. This would still be wildly unsafe, though: the average rural road has one car pass every ninety seconds, suggesting the couple would still be risking being run over six times. There are, it seems, very good reasons not to do it in the road. Also, gravel.

DO THE DRUGS WORK?

THE VERVE

Ashcroft, R., has clearly come to his own conclusion on whether the drugs work, decisively ruling that they do not, but it's not clear from the study alone what drugs are being assessed, or by what criteria they are being judged.

Many people believe the song is not, in fact, about recreational drug use, but instead refers to a dying cancer patient (at various points rumored to be Ashcroft's father-in-law). Though in that instance the drugs didn't work, they do work for many: a huge meta-analysis of 100,000 breast cancer patients found chemotherapy reduced ten-year mortality—the proportion of people who die within ten years of diagnosis—by a third, a huge success rate.

However, the song has in reality been confirmed by Ashcroft to be about recreational use of illegal drugs; indeed the use of the phrase "coming down" in reference to his own state of mind would suggest psychoactive stimulants being cleared from his system, resulting in dysphoria.

It is hard to gain data on the general efficacy of illegal drugs. And while they can usually be said to "work" in that they have the effects people buy them for, there are numerous reasons Ashcroft can use to justify his claim. Firstly, many drugs are either cut with chalk or even harmful substances, or sometimes replaced by them entirely—rendering them ineffective. Or, as Ashcroft suggests, the drug's negative effects quickly come to outweigh the good ones—though in this case Ashcroft would have been more lyrically and scientifically accurate if he had written, "The drugs might work / But their adverse / Effects far outweigh the benefits."

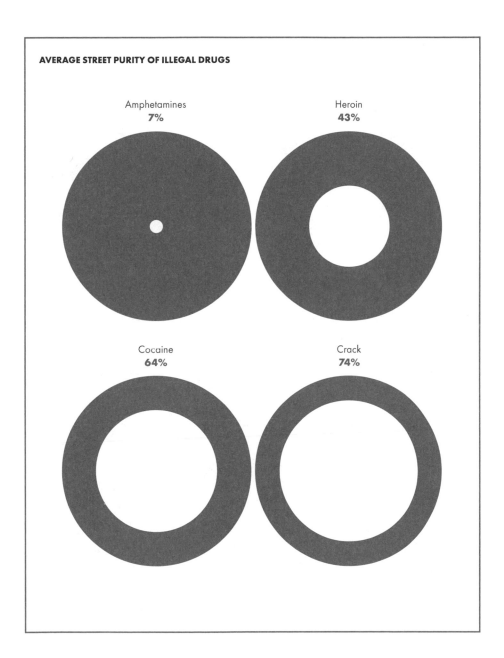

AVERAGE STREET PURITY OF ILLEGAL DRUGS

Amphetamines
7%

Heroin
43%

Cocaine
64%

Crack
74%

BICYCLES IN BEIJING

KEY

1 million bicycles

Official figures

Melua study

ARE THERE NINE MILLION BICYCLES IN BEIJING?

KATIE MELUA

When Melua, K., asserted the number of bikes in her 2005 study, she surely could not have been aware of the controversies it would cause in nerd communities—of which more later.

The titular claim is based on a long-standing belief, something of an urban myth, that there are 9 million bicycles in China's capital, Beijing. There is, in reality, no justification for the statistic, though it is plausible. Beijing is a city known for its bikes, and the city has a population of 22 million, making a total of 9 million cycles possible—but vanishingly unlikely. Chinese government statistics suggest 14 percent of people in the city frequently commute by bicycle, suggesting a total of around 2.1 million bicycles in regular use. The government is trying to increase this to 18 percent to tackle air pollution, which could add another 600,000 or so bikes to the city's roads—but still far short of Melua's far more ambitious calculation.

It was not the bicycles, though, that ignited controversy in the wake of the song's release. Melua also asserts during its course that the Earth is around 12 billion light-years from the edge of the universe—but she calls this a "guess," which no one can confirm the truth of.

This sparked the ire of theoretical physicist and science communicator Simon Singh, who defended his field by noting that the estimate of the Earth's distance from the edge of the universe is based on substantial scientific evidence. Eventually, Melua agreed to re-record a version of the lyric with phrasing that suited Singh better: "We are 13.7 billion light-years from the edge of the observable universe," runs Singh's suggested lyric. "That's a good estimate with well-defined error bars." It is perhaps unsurprising Singh is a physicist rather than a lyricist.

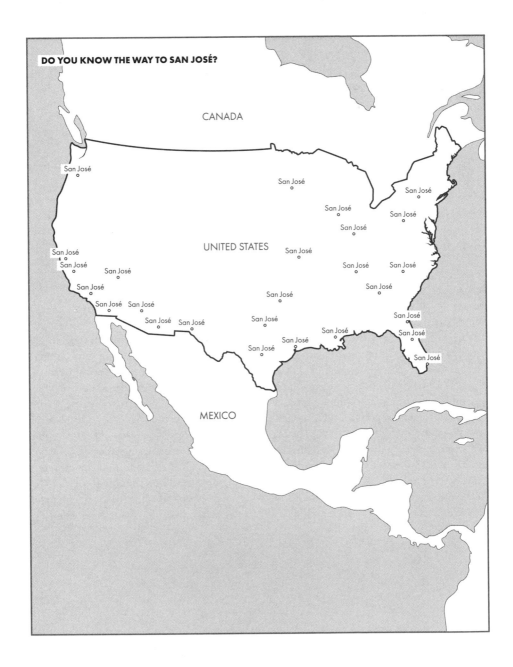

DO YOU KNOW THE WAY TO SAN JOSÉ?

DIONNE WARWICK

Warwick, D., describes an interesting situation. She urgently wants to get to San José, where she has lots of friends, believes she can find peace of mind, enjoys its space, and thinks she will easily find somewhere to stay. But despite knowing many people there, and even having been born and raised in the city, Warwick has found herself lost and unable to find her way to it—despite it being California's third-largest city.

We are forced to consider the interesting question of what it means to "know" the way somewhere. In a pretechnological age, it would be measured by someone's ability to find their way there, or indeed, describe how someone else might get there. However, in a modern world in which every smartphone is a map with GPS, this becomes more difficult to assess. But if we define "knowing the way" as relating only to knowledge in our brains, and not including any devices, then Warwick, D., will probably be disappointed.

Even if the passers-by she flags down know the way to San José, she is unlikely to be able to get comprehensible directions from them. This is due to a psychological effect known as the "curse of knowledge": we become able to get to a well-known destination on mental autopilot, and so we forget the conscious cues that remind us of how to get there—how to tell which of the four junctions is the one to make the left turn at, or even how many junctions there are before the correct turn.

The more worrying factor is that because of the plasticity of the brain—for example, we know that cab drivers who take "the knowledge test" about London streets show an increase in "gray matter" in their posterior hippocampus—it is not alarmist to suggest that if we don't use this part of our brain, it may eventually atrophy.

HOW WORRIED SHOULD YOU BE IF SOMEONE'S WATCHING YOU WITH THE EYE OF THE TIGER?

SURVIVOR

During the course of this investigation into survival technique, Jamison, J., is clearly describing the preparation for a major confrontation with a rival—one that he takes seriously, as he repeatedly warns those within earshot that they are being watched with the "eye of the tiger."

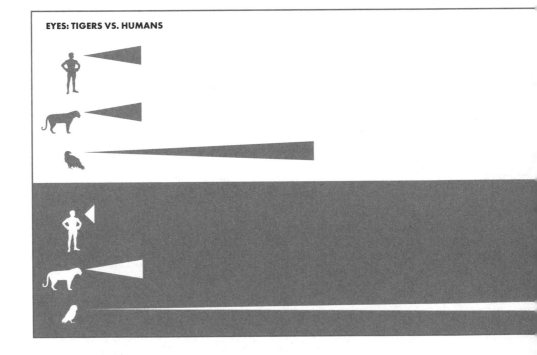

EYES: TIGERS VS. HUMANS

Jamison may be something of an unreliable narrator: he refers in one moment to the "last known survivor" before addressing a comment to "us all," suggesting either he is omitting essential context or else is hazy on the concept of a "final survivor." Setting this issue aside, though, it is credible that a human rival could be watching with the eye of a tiger: during daylight hours, the eyesight of a tiger is roughly equivalent to the sight of a typical human.

However, Jamison specifically refers to the song taking place at night, when humans would have far more reasons to worry about a tiger's sight: at night tigers' vision is around five or six times better than that of a human.

There could be far worse scenarios than being watched with tigers' eyes, though: if an opponent had the vision of an eagle, they would have daytime sight around eight times further than a human, with the ability to focus on a rabbit at a distance of two miles.

At night, owls' eyes would be a far greater worry: owls' eyes make up around 10,000 times more of their weight than human eyes do of theirs, have extraordinary ability to use low light, and have far greater density of light receptors.

Being watched by the eye of the tiger would be unnerving—but it could be so much worse.

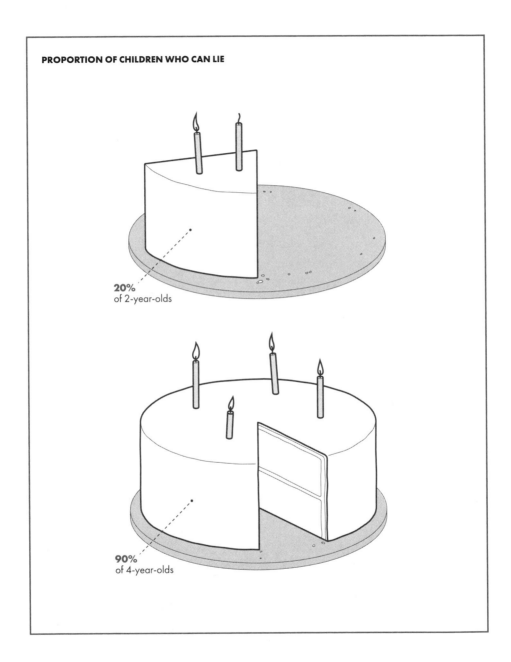

PROPORTION OF CHILDREN WHO CAN LIE

20%
of 2-year-olds

90%
of 4-year-olds

WOULD I LIE TO YOU?

CHARLES & EDDIE

In this 1992 report on the likelihood of an individual lying, it is proposed that truth can be assessed by the openness of a subject's eyes, with wide eyes posited as evidence of the truthfulness of their interactions with their "baby."

Though we can find no studies for the wideness of eyes and truthfulness, there has been a lot of research into whether eye movement reveals lies, with Professor Richard Wiseman of the University of Hertfordshire finding no relationship between lying and eye movements. In fact, verbal hesitations and excessive hand gestures may be a better guide. Pettigrew, C., and Chacon, E., are perhaps referring to this theory when they state that it is "in their arms" where we might find the "only truth," though they do not say what their arms are doing.

However, we can look at the likelihood of Pettigrew and Chacon lying in another way. Research in 2010 by academics at Michigan State University found that 60 percent of respondents said they had told no lies whatsoever in the previous 24 hours, and found that half of all the lies reported in the survey of 1,000 adults had come from just 5 percent of respondents. There is one problem with that research, however: people might lie about lying.

We learn how to lie at a very early age. Researchers at Toronto's Institute of Child Study told children not to peek at a toy behind their backs when alone (but recorded) in a room. At the age of two, only 20 percent of children were able to lie about whether they peeked, but by age four, 90 percent could lie about that (and lying didn't peak until the children reached the age of twelve). For humans, lying is second nature.

We continue to lie as adults: the University of Massachusetts asked 121 undergraduates to talk to a stranger and try to appear either likable or competent, and secretly recorded them. They then asked the students to identify if they'd lied at all during the conversation. To even their own surprise, more than 60 percent of respondents found they'd lied at least once, often without even being aware of it.

This spells a problem for Pettigrew and Chacon: not only might we be unable to tell if they're lying to us, they might not even know it themselves.

HOW MUCH WOULD YOU HAVE TO EARN TO BE "BARELY GETTIN' BY" IN LA IN 1980?

DOLLY PARTON

Parton, D., makes a vital contribution to our understanding of the psychology and economics of low-quality work. While endless column inches are filled with stories about how millennials want more from the workplace than previous generations, Parton was ahead of the curve. In 1980 she vividly documents nine-to-five jobs that didn't give due credit, took without giving, and shattered dreams.

She also flagged the roles paid only just enough to "get by"—but didn't specify what level of income that was. Fortunately, we can calculate it: during this period, Parton was based in California, which at the time had a minimum wage of $3.10 an hour. Assuming she worked a typical five-day week with a daily unpaid lunch hour, that would give her a weekly income of $108.50 and annual earnings of $5,642 pretax.

The US has historically set much stricter definitions of poverty than other countries, and Parton's 35-hour week would see her comfortably above its 1980 threshold of $3,400 for a single person. If we wanted a more generous definition of "barely getting by"—such as the international threshold of 60 percent of average earnings—Parton would fall far short, as this line would be around $7,500.

To earn that—a rough approximation of getting by—she'd have to have her wages hiked to $4.10 or so, which seems unlikely under her current line-management structure. However, it would probably provoke envy in many low-earning US families today to imagine you could get by on just one job. Recent studies suggest that as many as 7.6 million workers, or 2.5 percent of the country, are working more than one job.

As it stands, Parton is doing far better than that: her net worth is today approximately $500 million. And so too are others. In 1985, when Parton was seeking support for her theme park Dollywood from the Pigeon Forge City Commission in East Tennessee, a spokesperson guaranteed that all staff would be paid above minimum wage.

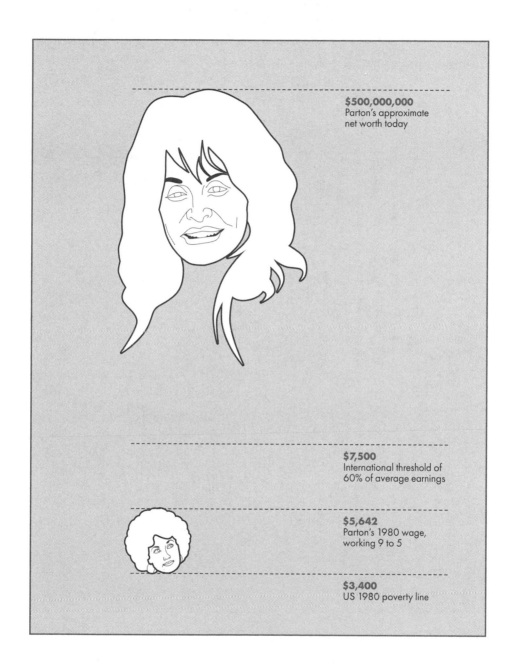

$500,000,000
Parton's approximate
net worth today

$7,500
International threshold of
60% of average earnings

$5,642
Parton's 1980 wage,
working 9 to 5

$3,400
US 1980 poverty line

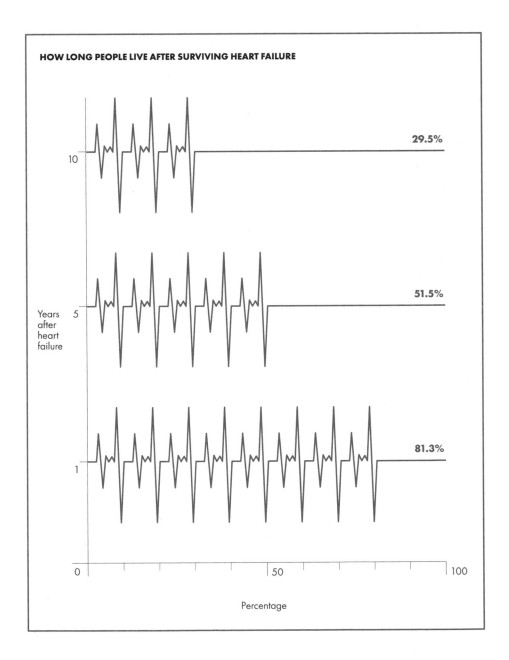

HOW LONG PEOPLE LIVE AFTER SURVIVING HEART FAILURE

29.5%

51.5%

Years after heart failure

81.3%

10

5

1

0   50   100

Percentage

WHAT BECOMES OF THE BROKENHEARTED?

JIMMY RUFFIN

Ruffin, J., changed cardiology forever in 1966 with his deep examination of what happened to those who survive coronary episodes.

Ruffin also shows some enlightenment as to the difficulty of improving such survival rates, singing of searching for solutions but not succeeding, and worrying that all remains are unhappy endings.

Ruffin's concerns are matched by the clinical evidence into what becomes of the brokenhearted, which we take to mean those who have suffered heart failure. Researchers collected evidence of the outcomes of 54,313 people in the UK who'd had heart attacks over the age of forty-five, and looked at their one-year, five-year, and ten-year survival rates.

The study found that 81.3 percent of the people studied were still alive after one year, 51.5 percent were still going five years later, and 29.5 percent—less than one in three—were still alive a decade after their first heart failure. Worse still, those survival rates had not improved over the fourteen-year period of the analysis.

It should be noted, though, that these figures looked much better for the relatively young patients in the group, more than 80 percent of whom survive five years, and more than two-thirds of whom were still alive after a decade. Ruffin's study courageously drew the public's attention to these serious issues, so if—as he stated—he is looking for peace of mind, perhaps he can find some there.

WHO'S TO BLAME: THE SUNSHINE, MOONLIGHT, GOOD TIMES, OR BOOGIE?

THE JACKSONS

This 1978 report explored the impact of boogie on a variety of issues, including the lack of "lovin'" and the authors' reduced ability to control their feet.

If boogie were entitled to a good defense lawyer, it would have a great chance of getting this inquisition called as a mistrial: from the very outset of the song—even from its very title—the Jacksons have decided what they are going to blame for the problems affecting them. However, one might find it an unusual

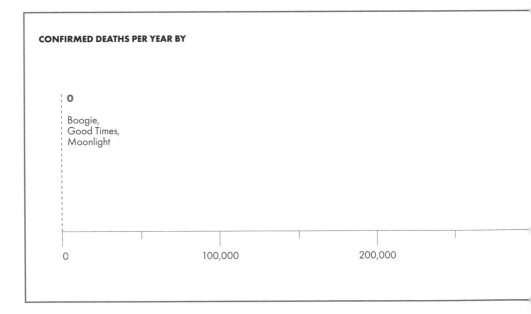

CONFIRMED DEATHS PER YEAR BY

0

Boogie,
Good Times,
Moonlight

0   100,000   200,000

use of everyone's time to try to assess whether dancing is to blame for people dancing.

Proper examination of the suspects the Jacksons list suggests they should not have jumped so rapidly to conclusions. While moonlight is largely blameless—though poor light at nighttime is not without hazards—good times and sunshine both come with major risks.

The USA's CDC estimates that good times, or at least the binge drinking that comes with them, cost the United States around $191 billion each year. The World Health Organization, meanwhile, estimates that the sun kills 60,000 people per year. That's some serious prior form that the Jacksons disregard entirely—all while boogying seems largely blameless.

The modern origins of the word *boogie* can be found in nineteenth-century jazz culture, and before that "boogie-woogie" was originally used to describe the symptoms of secondary syphilis in slave slang. Boogie meant a slave, and "boogeyman" went on to become a generic title for a scary individual, possibly linked to the idea of escaped slaves hiding. That usage can be traced back to the French word *bougre*, which, roughly translated, means a "guy" or "chap," from which we get the word *bugger*; and before that to the French *boulgre*, which referred to a sect of eleventh-century Bulgarian heretics.

In its modern form, boogying is good exercise: a study at Harvard University suggests a person of average weight would burn around 205 calories in 30 minutes of disco dancing, versus just 112 for a waltz or fox-trot. Perhaps this is why the Jacksons called for a last-minute reprieve of the boogie: deciding that we should only blame ourselves.

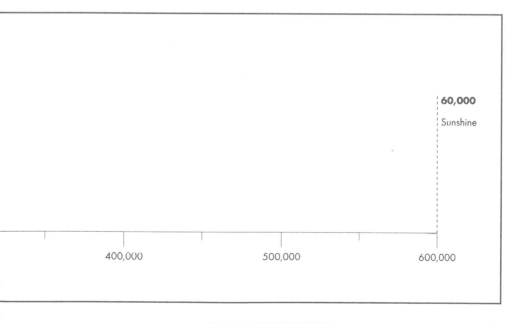

ARE YOU TELLING ME THIS IS A SIGN?

SNOOP DOGG

The two principal contributors to this study, Messrs. Timberlake, J., and Dogg, S., disagree—some might say to a problematic extent—about whether or not a particular woman is flirting with one or both of them.

Their primary method of assessment is whether or not she's looking in their eyes. That the two of them find it difficult to detect whether or not the unnamed woman is flirting, though, should not come as a surprise: humans are terrible at detecting when someone is flirting with us.

One attempt to try to establish how good we are at perceiving flirting was published in the journal *Communication Research* in 2014. The academics matched up heterosexual strangers into fifty-two pairs, and asked them to talk for around ten to twelve minutes. Each participant was then asked afterward whether or not they had been flirting (meaning it relied on self-reporting), and whether they thought their partner was flirting.

The results suggested that we are generally quite good at detecting when someone is not flirting with us: cases where someone thought their conversational partner was flirting when they were not were rare. However, that accuracy dropped markedly when the other person was indeed flirting: this was often missed.

The pattern held true when other people were watching the recorded interactions—people could generally tell when flirting wasn't taking place, but often missed when it was. However, there is some reassurance for Dogg, S., and Timberlake, J.: generally, participants found it easier to tell when a woman was flirting than when a man was.

AM I A CREEP?

RADIOHEAD

The author of this 1993 case study, Yorke, T., proceeds from the premise that he is a creep.

It is our assertion, though, that he reaches this conclusion with very little empirical evidence and merely creates two false categories: "creep" and "f---in' special" into one of which he must fall. There is evidence that someone's skin making you cry could be construed as creepy but it's certainly not conclusive.

A study published in the journal *New Ideas in Psychology* in 2016—twenty-four years after the song's release—declared itself the first empirical study of "creepiness." The study, which involved 1,341 people across the world, found that overall men were seen as more likely to be creepy than women, and that (unsurprisingly) women associated sexual threat—the risk of being unsafe—with creepiness.

The research did also come up with some specific jobs and behaviors that correlated with creepiness. The four creepiest professions were clown, taxidermist, sex shop owner, and funeral director—while farmers, teachers, and meteorologists were at the bottom of the scale.

When it comes to appearances associated with creepiness, unkempt hair, pale skin, bags under the eyes, and "odd" or dirty clothing all registered, while types of behavior deemed creepy included steering the conversation to one topic, standing too close, and licking lips.

The research provides some good clues for Yorke's character in the case study: with the right occupation, dirty clothing, and inappropriate social behavior, he can be the creep he believes himself to be. Or if not, clean clothes and hair, standing further away, and becoming a farmer could address the issue in no time.

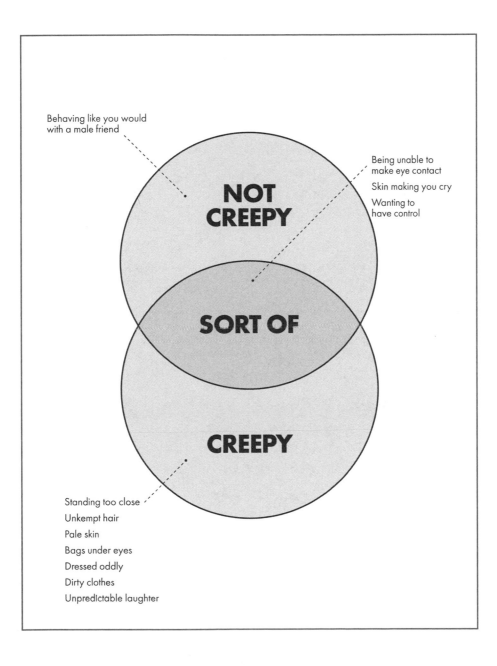

Behaving like you would
with a male friend

NOT
CREEPY

Being unable to
make eye contact

Skin making you cry

Wanting to
have control

SORT OF

CREEPY

Standing too close
Unkempt hair
Pale skin
Bags under eyes
Dressed oddly
Dirty clothes
Unpredictable laughter

London

Northern Scotland

KEY

1 White
Christmas

DID WE USED TO KNOW WHITE CHRISTMASES?

BING CROSBY

Crosby, B., made his seminal contribution to festive meteorology in 1942, in a song in which he implies that the frequency of white Christmases have declined since he was an adult.

Crosby, B., had good reason to be nostalgic for white Christmases. Having grown up in Spokane, in Washington State, more than two-thirds of his childhood Christmases would have seen snow, giving him good reason to fondly miss such weather conditions—though given he decided to live in California as an adult, he should perhaps not have been surprised to see fewer snowstorms.

Whether Crosby was justified in spreading his nostalgia to the wider world, however, is more questionable: despite our treacherous memories, many of us in the US and UK alike will have grown up with fewer white Christmases than we might think.

While in states like Alaska and Minnesota the chance of a white Christmas on any given year is 90 percent or more, much of the continental US experiences a very different story.

Despite its famed association with the festive season, New York City has just one in five white Christmases, Philadelphia just one in ten, and Hawaii has, unsurprisingly, never experienced one.

This is similarly true in the UK: southern England has experienced just ten white Christmases in the last fifty-seven years, versus thirty out of fifty-seven in northern Scotland. The UK is also hampered by an odd official definition of "white Christmas": the Meteorological Office defines a Christmas as white if its sensors pick up a single snowflake, even if it doesn't settle on the ground—meaning 2015 counted as a white Christmas, despite no settled snow anywhere in the country. This may satisfy a formal definition, but there is a reason why Crosby did not wish our Christmases to be merry, bright, and "white, but only on a technicality."

ANIMALS AND THEIR MEMORY ABILITIES

5.6 billion
African elephant

0.245 billion
Marmoset

1.7 billion
Rhesus monkey

9.1 billion
Gorilla

6 billion
Chimpanzee

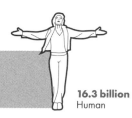

16.3 billion
Human

Cerebral cortex neurons

WHAT ABOUT ELEPHANTS—HAVE WE LOST THEIR TRUST?

MICHAEL JACKSON

In his plea for us to have greater levels of care for the world, Jackson, M., poses a question that biologists have sought to work out for over two decades: Have we lost elephants' trust?

Elephants certainly have good reasons to mistrust humanity: a study published in the journal of the USA's National Academy found that poachers killed one in twelve of all living African elephants in 2011 alone, and have killed two-thirds of the elephants in central Africa in the course of a decade. Across the continent, researchers estimate poachers killed no fewer than 100,000 elephants in just three years.

Given that track record, elephants would have good reason to be wary, if they're bright enough to pick up on the warning signs. Research on forty-seven elephants by two academics at the University of Sussex found that elephants can distinguish between different tribes of people and respond differently depending on whether that tribe does or does not hunt elephants.

Not only did the elephants distinguish between tribes by smell and by clothing, they can distinguish language: when the animals were played calm recordings from Maasai tribesmen (who sometimes kill elephants) they panicked and huddled, and when they heard recordings from Kamba tribesmen (who very rarely kill elephants), they did not.

That suggests Jackson was right to question if we have lost elephants' trust. At least some of us have, but given what's happening to their populations, they should perhaps trust us even less than they do.

100
Another human

96
Chimpanzee

90
Cat

85
Mouse

61
Fruit Fly

POP SCIENCE

WHAT COMPARES TO YOU?

SINEAD O'CONNOR

O'Connor, S., builds upon original research by Rogers Nelson, P., in this investigation into the comparative value of an individual over time.

This was a tightly measured survey, taking place fifteen days and seven hours after an unnamed individual has left. O'Connor's thesis—that her former beau was incomparable—does not stand up well to scrutiny, however, even within her own internal logic, as she refers to avoiding other boys as they'd remind her of him, suggesting that they were indeed comparable. It is implied that her former lover stopped her from eating her dinner in fancy restaurants, and we're told he planted flowers in the backyard—two things that are unlikely to be impossible to find in another individual.

More broadly, in literature lovers have been compared to innumerable things, perhaps most famously to "a summer's day" by Shakespeare (even if the bard then decided the comparison was a poor one as the lover to whom it was addressed would last far longer than a summery day).

In scientific terms, we are especially comparable: most humans arc 99.9 percent genetically similar to one another, as well as 96 percent comparable with a chimpanzee, 90 percent with a cat, 85 percent with a mouse, and even 61 percent with a fly. So we are quite comparable even to things that seem very different from us.

This gets even more striking when humans are considered on a chemical level: 96 percent of our body mass is made up of oxygen, carbon, hydrogen, and nitrogen. Those are the same chemicals that make up (in different mixtures) many of the things around us—the air, the sea, and much else. Biologically and scientifically, almost everything compares to you. Perhaps the only thing that cannot be compared to a human is the vacuum of space, or "nothing," although even then both us and nothing are bathing in the cosmic background microwave radiation from the Big Bang so are technically comparable, leaving us with the real answer that even nothing compares to you.

DO YOU LIKE PIÑA COLADAS, AND GETTING CAUGHT IN THE RAIN?

RUPERT HOLMES

In this song, Holmes, R., sets out the story of how he planned to cheat on his girlfriend with a woman who later turns out in fact to be his girlfriend, because he had (accidentally) seen a very specific advert she had placed in the newspaper's personal ads column, and he felt it matched him perfectly.

Holmes recounts the advert's requirements in the song's first chorus: the man being sought by the then unknown woman must like piña coladas, like being rained on, dislike yoga, be relatively intelligent ("have half a brain") and like making love on a beach.

Thanks to research by YouGov carried out on 1,641 UK adults for this book, we can calculate how many matches she could expect from her advert: 34 percent of men like piña coladas, 27 percent like getting caught in rain, 81 percent aren't interested in yoga, 80 percent think of themselves as intelligent, and 34 percent say they enjoy sex on beaches. That means overall around 2 percent of men would match all five requirements on the advert—meaning even in a small town like Northwich, Cheshire (Holmes's hometown), she could expect 753 potential matches. As such, Holmes should count himself lucky that he saw the personal advert before any of his 752 would-be rivals did.

PERCENTAGES OF UK MEN WHO...

34% Like piña coladas

27% Like getting caught in the rain

81% Dislike yoga

80% Consider themselves to have half a brain

34% Like making love on the dunes

2% Match all five requirements

PERCENTAGE OF CELLS IN YOUR BODY WHICH ARE:

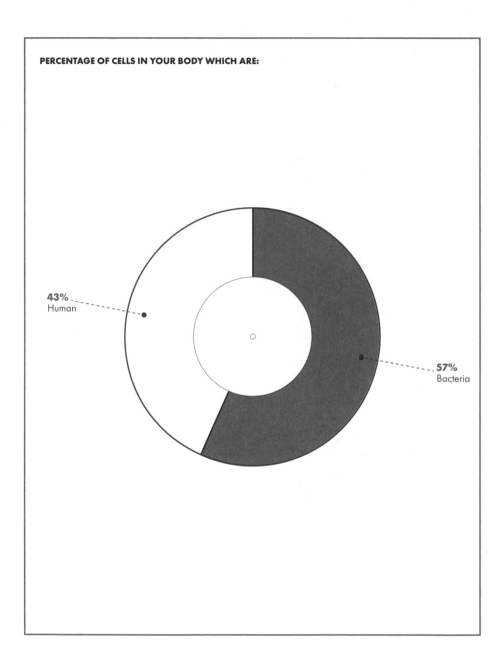

43%
Human

57%
Bacteria

POP SCIENCE

ARE YOU LONESOME TONIGHT?

ELVIS PRESLEY

Even a casual observer of Presley, E.'s, apparently solicitous concern about the loneliness or otherwise of the object of his treatise would notice that it is laced with self-interest.

Despite initial appearances, the real aim of Presley's inquiries rapidly becomes clear: he wants to know whether he is being missed, whether the house seems empty, whether his correspondent is still in love with him.

Survey data published in *Glamour* magazine would offer some limited comfort to Presley, and perhaps save him the effort of wondering so extensively. These figures suggested that Presley's paramour may have been thinking of him, as 54 percent of people said they'd had second thoughts about a breakup, but while people may have had regrets, not many wanted to act on them. Only 22 percent said they had found it difficult to move on from an ex, and only 19 percent said they found it difficult to move on once their ex had a new partner.

While there is a statistically even chance that Presley's former partner would be feeling lonesome, there is virtually zero chance that they would be utterly alone—though the company may not be human.

Almost every adult across the world plays host to at least one or two breeds of other creatures. Most of us would hope not to provide accommodation to fleas or ticks, and thankfully most of us don't. What almost all of us host are two breeds of mites called demodex. The biggest of the two is known as demodex folliculorum, which are around half a millimeter long and live primarily in the hair follicles on your face—in your eyelashes, cheeks, chin, and more, feeding off sweat and dead skin in biweekly cycles. We have almost none of these while we're children (to the age of ten), but almost every adult will eventually get them—up to five per hair follicle in healthy people.

Meanwhile, we're also outnumbered in our bodies by bacteria: we have around 30 trillion cells in our body but play host to 39 trillion bacteria. So while we might feel lonesome, and miss human company and conversation, we're never truly alone.

WHAT DOES THE FOX SAY?

YLVIS

In 2014, four relatively unknown contributors known as Ylvis attempted to answer the question of what the fox says.

The first verse of their song displays a reasonable knowledge of the animal kingdom, accurately identifying the noises made by dogs, cats, birds, cows, frogs, and more—though their assertion that fish go "blub" is problematic. However, things appear to take a wrong turn when they attempt to answer the central question of what foxes say.

The singers offer up a range of options, from "ring-ding-ding," to "wa-pa-pa," "cha cha cha," and "fraka-kaka." None of the options, as anyone who lives in a city with a decent population of urban foxes will tell you, is remotely accurate: foxes don't say all that much, except in January—and at that point they are loud.

Foxes have their mating season around January, and during this relatively short period of the year they will wake up people during the night as their courtship rituals are distinctive. As a male is making his approach, the female will let out a number of loud, almost human-like shrieks (which occasionally result in calls to police).

Once mating begins, the genitals of the male and female lock together, for between twenty minutes and one hour (because fox sperm swims slowly), making it physically impossible for the animals to separate from each other. During this time, the female makes a lengthy, almost unworldly shriek not easily conveyed by text. Researchers believe the sex to be nonpainful, but the noise appears anything but: it sounds entirely possible that the vixen at least is saying "ouch, my cervix."

ISN'T IT IRONIC?	IRONIC	NOT IRONIC
Being afraid of flying, overcoming it, and dying in a crash	✔	
10,000 spoons when a knife is needed		✘
Meeting a dream man who's married		✘
Winning the lottery and immediately dying		✘
A fly in your wine		✘
Death row pardons arriving late		✘
Rain at a wedding		✘
Being offered a free ride after paying		✘
TOTAL	*1*	*7*

ISN'T IT IRONIC, DON'T YOU THINK?

ALANIS MORISSETTE

In this landmark 1995 semantic survey, Morissette, A., conducts a thorough analysis of the concept of irony, typically defined as circumstances working the opposite of what they would be expected to, usually in such a way as to provoke amusement.

Morissette's study has proven controversial for decades as, despite offering numerous examples of irony to explain the concept to her audience, most or all of them fail, in reality, to be ironic. Rain on a wedding day is inconvenient but not ironic, unless both bride and groom are meteorologists specializing in short-term precipitation forecasting. Finding a surplus of thousands of spoons while searching for a single knife is irritating, but again not an irony, unless you are a cutlery spokesperson looking for a knife to open the envelope of your newly delivered forecast of high-knife versus low-spoon yield in the current quarter. Falling in love with a man only to discover he's married is a fairly common occurrence. A death row pardon arriving after the execution has begun is tragic, but again fails to meet the threshold for irony, unless perhaps you are on death row for murdering the founder of a faster courier service for death row pardons.

This long-standing controversy actually provoked Morissette to offer a retraction of her study two decades later, in 2015, when she stated "there are no ironies." However, this retraction has an issue: the initial study did, in fact, contain one irony.

Morissette set out the case study of a man afraid of flight who was finally convinced to take a plane—only for it to crash. Statistically, the man was wise to take the flight: only one in 3,000,000 flights result in a crash with fatalities, while motorbiking is 3,000 times more dangerous mile for mile than flying, driving is 100 times deadlier, and even trains are twice as deadly. So Morissette's example showed a man rationally losing his fear of flight, only to become the rare exception—he had been correct.

The syntax of Morissette's question is also ambiguous: "Do not you think this is ironic?" So this does risk making her retraction incorrect. Isn't that ironic? We think. It's hard to tell at this point.

WHAT IS LOVE?

HADDAWAY

In this key investigation of 1993, Haddaway, N., seeks to address two issues, one philosophical—what is love?—and one more immediate: he would like his baby to stop hurting him. We should tackle the philosophical problem first, as trying to describe what love is has plagued poets and writers for millennia.

A good starting point for Haddaway would be to ignore said poets. As any good social scientist knows, their approach to these kinds of definitional questions are imprecise and unhelpful. We can also discern from the context of the song, and specifically from his pleas for monogamy, that Haddaway is not referring to platonic love, or parental love, but rather romantic love. Other comparable studies involve Gibb, B., Gibb, R., and Gibb M., who attempted to answer the question of how deep love is by pinpointing the exact areas of the brain where love is found, and the Black Eyed Peas, who attempted, unsuccessfully, to answer the more general question, "Where is the love?"

However, perhaps the most helpful answer for Haddaway is that "love" is a societal shorthand for a combination of physiological responses and sociological behaviors: it is the hormonal reaction that we feel as lust or desire, coupled with a relationship of trust and affection built over time, laced with sociological expectations such as monogamy, expectations of gender roles, and more.

Having addressed Haddaway's first issue with his romantic partner, we need to consider his parental nonsequitur: if his infant is hurting him—especially at such a young age—he should seek immediate advice from a qualified child psychologist.

10 USEFUL LOVE WORDS THAT HAVE NO DIRECT TRANSLATION IN ENGLISH

IKTSUARPOK
INUIT

The joyous anticipation you feel
when you're waiting for someone
you love to come to your house.

FENSTERLN
GERMAN

The act of climbing through a
window to have sex with someone,
so their parents won't know about it.

SAUDADE
PORTUGUESE

An intense longing for a person
or place you love but is now lost.
A desire for that which is gone.

KARA SEVDE
TURKISH

Literally means "black love." The description
of being so lovesick through passion that
you become blind to a person's faults.

YA'ABURNEE
ARABIC

Literally translated as "you bury me."
The hope you will die before the
person you love so that you don't
have to live without them.

**KOI NO
YOKAN**
JAPANESE

The sudden intimation that the
person you have just met is
someone you will fall in love with.

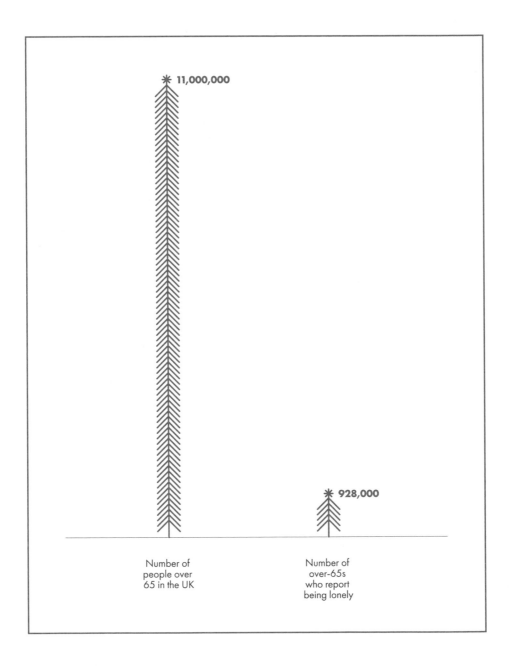

✳ 11,000,000

✳ 928,000

Number of
people over
65 in the UK

Number of
over-65s
who report
being lonely

WILL IT BE LONELY THIS CHRISTMAS?

MUD

In 1974, Chapman, M., and Chinn, N., investigated whether it would be lonely this Christmas.

Though the study was rooted in one specific instance of a partner leaving, and particularly the attendant issues surrounding temperature—it's taken as a given that the absence of the partner will negatively impact the ability of the individual to regulate their body temperature. Leaving this spurious correlation aside, the report's authors hit on a sad social reality for thousands of people. Looking at their home country of the UK, research by Age UK in 2017 found that 928,000 older people feel lonelier around the time of Christmas, with around 370,000 of those feeling lonely in part because they had been widowed.

While making what can only have been intended as an earnest and deliberate effort to draw attention to this plight, Chapman and Chinn's warning that it would be cold without a partner at Christmas can be seen as a slight exaggeration.

While some older people do struggle with this, pensioners are now the least likely group in the UK to be in poverty, and even receive extra winter payments for heating—meaning that, hopefully, despite what Chapman and Chinn say, they should not be cold.

However, if Chapman and Chinn's words have drawn your attention to the issue and you wish to make Christmas less lonely, you can take a look at ageuk.org.uk/get-involved in the UK or friendtofriendamerica.org in the US.

WHY'D YOU HAVE TO GO AND MAKE THINGS SO COMPLICATED?

AVRIL LAVIGNE

Lavigne, A., set out in 2002 a series of concerns regarding a close associate with whom she'd previously been able to communicate clearly and simply—especially when the two were driving together—whereas now things have become "complicated" and he is behaving oddly enough that she speculates he is acting like somebody else, exhibiting paranoia and a performative selfhood, and she is finding the whole situation extremely frustrating.

Lavigne had to wait a decade for psychological research to confirm the likely cause of her situation, but in 2012 answers finally came in the form of the academic paper "Evidence for the Pinocchio Effect: Linguistic Differences Between Lies, Deception by Omission, and Truths," which used experiments to discern the differences in language used by people telling the truth, leaving something out, or downright lying.

The study examined what it called the "Pinocchio effect"—the tendency for liars to use more words, and so tell a more elaborate story, than people telling the truth—and found this effect existed. When matched with an unwitting partner, liars used 76 words on average, versus 32.5 for truth-tellers and just 30 for those lying by omission.

Liars, the research showed, also used more third-person pronouns, more numbers, and more profanities than their truth-telling counterparts, while other studies have found that liars take fractionally longer to respond to a question than a truth-teller does, because lying puts more cognitive load on the brain than telling the truth—you have to think up which lie to tell, rather than telling the one extant truth. In a very real sense, lies make things more complicated in your brain.

Why did he have to make things so complicated? The likely explanation is because he was telling lies. Still, given 40 percent of adults admit to lying once per day, Lavigne was correct to note that "life's like this."

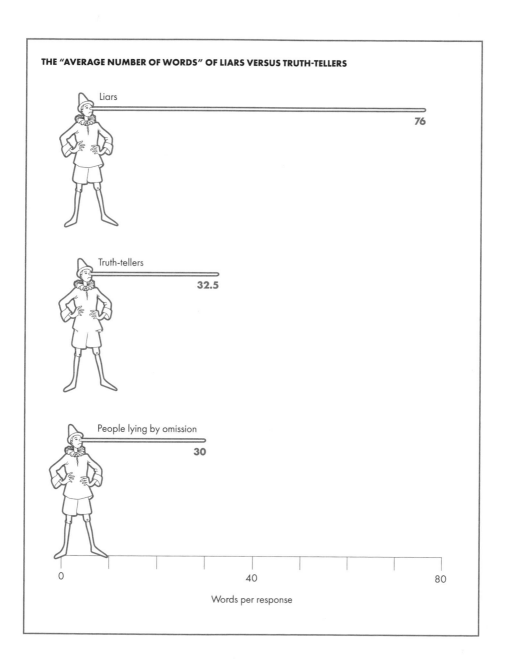

THE "AVERAGE NUMBER OF WORDS" OF LIARS VERSUS TRUTH-TELLERS

Liars

76

Truth-tellers

32.5

People lying by omission

30

0   40   80

Words per response

WHERE ARE YOUR FRIENDS TONIGHT?

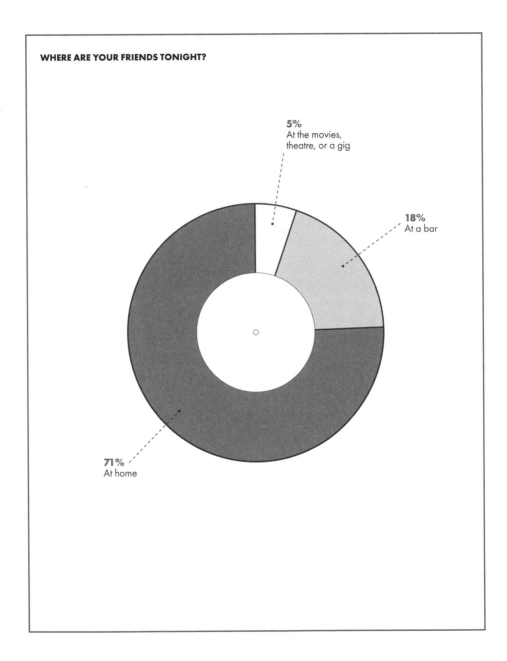

5%
At the movies,
theatre, or a gig

18%
At a bar

71%
At home

WHERE ARE YOUR FRIENDS TONIGHT?

LCD SOUNDSYSTEM

In this qualitative study, Murphy, J., and his colleagues set out to pose—rather than answer—a question regarding the location of people's associates during an evening.

Such data would clearly be valuable for a number of uses, including perhaps a study of the nighttime economy, planning public transport requirements, and even the most efficient deployment of emergency service resources.

Murphy is also clearly primarily interested in the nocturnal interests of people as they get older, referring at various points to "the ways we show our age," having a "face like a dad," and even speaking of feeling "finally dead" when kids are just too "impossibly tanned."

However, Murphy never actually makes the attempt to gather the evidence on where the aforementioned friends are that night, leaving the window open for this author—who is now in his thirties—to attempt to further this research.

An initial attempt to quantify the whereabouts of friends on September 22, 2017, was thwarted by more than a third of those considered being in the company of LCD Soundsystem, leading to the study being dismissed due to sample bias (it heavily overindexed on North London media workers).

A repeat study was carried out some months later, polling 968 Twitter users who follow the author on where they would be at 10pm that Friday night. The results were reassuring for those who worry their friends have more fun than they do: 71 percent of respondents said they would be "at home" at that time, while 18 percent said they would be at a bar, and just 5 percent would be at the movies, theatre, or a gig.

Where are your friends tonight? They're most likely by some margin to be at home.

WHAT'S COOLER THAN BEING COOL?

OUTKAST

This research collaboration by 3000, A., and Patton, A., has perhaps become more famous for its errata than for its findings.

Notably, the collaborators suggested it was advisable to "shake it like a Polaroid picture," which prompted Polaroid to release a statement reminding their customers that Polaroids should not be shaken while their image develops. Sadly, due to a lack of postpublication clarification, we cannot establish whether 3000 and Patton were in fact recommending that people remain entirely still, or whether they just have a poor understanding of the chemical processes of Polaroid photography.

However, we also wish to tackle the second research question addressed by 3000 and Patton, regarding coolness. For the average person, a temperature range that would be regarded as "cool" but not "cold" would be around 54°F to 59°F. This leaves a wide range of temperatures available to answer the core question.

3000 and Patton offer up their own answer of "ice cold." While correct, we feel this solution is too narrow in scope, as water freezes at around 32°F—leaving temperatures both higher and lower that could correctly be called cooler than cool.

The lowest recorded temperature on Earth, for example, is –128.6°F, which was observed at a Soviet weather station in the Antarctic, but we can get far colder than this. Liquid nitrogen is generally at a temperature between –330°F and –321°F, whereas "absolute zero"—the lowest possible temperature—has been calculated at –460°F.

So while "ice cold" is accurate, a better answer would be "any temperature in the range of –460°F to 54°F." An even shorter answer would be "loads of stuff."

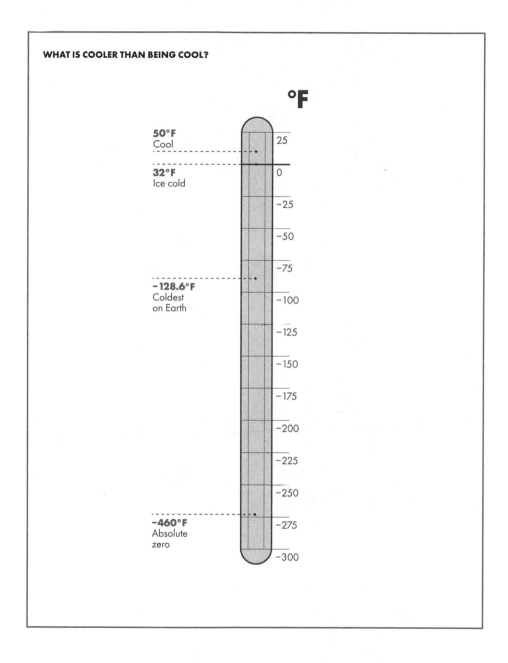

°**F**

50°F
Cool

25

32°F
Ice cold

0

−25

−50

−75

−128.6°F
Coldest
on Earth

−100

−125

−150

−175

−200

−225

−250

−460°F
Absolute
zero

−275

−300

22,236 mi
Geostationary satellites

400–700 mi
Low earth
orbit satellites

373 mi
The Hubble
space telescope

200 mi
The minimum height
for a satellite to
avoid atmospheric
interference

62 mi
The Kármán line—
space begins

0 mi
Sea level

5.5 mi
Mount Everest

5.68 mi
Commercial flights

WHY DO YOU ONLY CALL ME WHEN YOU'RE HIGH?

ARCTIC MONKEYS

It should perhaps come as no surprise that the team behind this study—Turner, A., et al.—are from Yorkshire, where hills and valleys coupled with a large rural population mean that phone signals are often difficult to access.

In rural Yorkshire, the question behind this study almost answers itself: people can only make calls when they're high because there's no signal in the valley. This is a popular belief that is supported by science. FM transmitters work by something quite close to line-of-sight: if there are obstacles (such as hills or buildings) between the transmitter and the radio, the signal quality descends sharply.

Phone signals are slightly more robust than this, but are also significantly affected by the distance from the transmitter and the obstacles in between. This, coupled with a reluctance from UK companies to fund phone towers in lightly populated valleys, means that signals in rural lowlands are terrible—seriously limiting their potential for phone calls.

There is one significant caveat for those wanting to make use of this advice in emergency situations, though: if you are, for example, lost in the wilderness, experts caution against seeking high ground to call for help if conditions are bad. As the Grand Canyon's chief of emergency services said to *Popular Mechanics* magazine, if you're climbing a rock formation for better signal during a storm, "you're just exposing yourself to risk." Do call for help when you're high—but make sure it's safe first.

WHERE IS 24 HOURS FROM TULSA?

GENE PITNEY

Those studying infidelity in the 1960s can find a compelling case study in correspondence from Pitney, G., who informed his partner by letter that he would not be seeing her anymore because he had cheated on her while only "24 hours" from their home in Tulsa, Oklahoma.

Clues as to Pitney's location at the point when he made this declaration—and when he cheated—can be found from his referral to the fact that he was "driving home." Given Tulsa's relatively central location within the US, this means there are a range of areas that are exactly a 24-hour drive from his destination.

He could, for example, have gotten to the delightful city of Manchester in New Hampshire, high in the northeast of the country. But it is hard to see why, beyond the unlikelihood of seeing anyone he knows, Pitney, G., would choose this location. He could have traveled to what has since become known as the Big Sky Colony in rural Montana, but which was then the Milford Hutterites—a US offshoot of the Hutterian Brethren, the Austrian branch of the Anabaptist movement of the sixteenth century who believed in communal living.

However, this seems an unlikely source for a partner in adultery.

The most likely location, it appears, is the notorious pleasure city of Reno, Nevada—exactly 1,657 miles and a 24-hour drive from Tulsa (and also only an hour or two away from San José, should he run into Warwick, D). Disaster could, perhaps, have been averted if Pitney had taken another form of transport: had he chosen to fly he could have been back in Tulsa in just five hours, with a connection in the famously morally upright Salt Lake City.

Given Pitney is now seeking to avoid retribution from his former partner, there are many ways in which he could get far further from Tulsa to somewhere remote—if he hopped to the airport, he could get 6,460 miles away to the very isolated Falkland Islands in 23 hours and 31 minutes, leaving himself 29 minutes to spare.

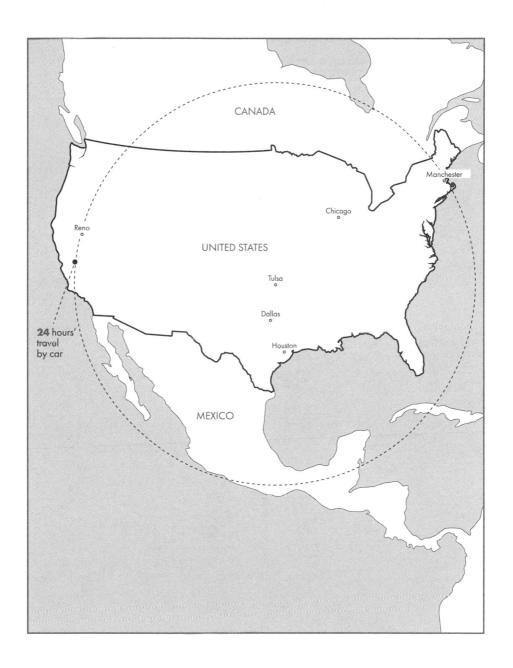

24 HOURS FROM TULSA

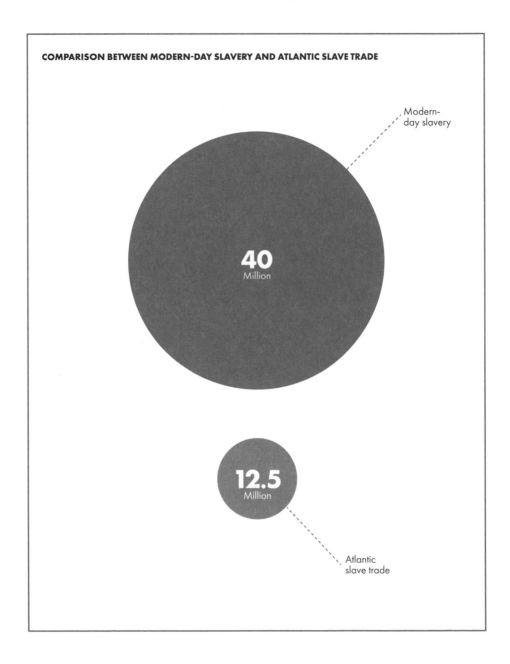

Modern-day slavery

40
Million

12.5
Million

Atlantic slave trade

OH CAN'T YOU SEE YOU BELONG TO ME?

THE POLICE

In this chilling public service announcement, Sumner, G., issues a serious and pressing warning about the perils of modern-day slavery, especially against the backdrop of current surveillance technology.

The limits of slavery are explicit and relate to every breath, move, step, and even, cruelly, each bond broken (which clearly refers to the possibility of escape being thwarted). Also, every word said, every day and night, every game played, every move made, vow broken, smile faked and claim staked—the all-seeing eye of cheap, available spying technology has drastically changed the dynamic of the slave trade.

During the course of the transatlantic slave trade, around 12.5 million people were shipped across the ocean into slavery—a figure now dwarfed by the levels of modern-day slavery, which is estimated to affect around 40 million people. Of those, around 25 million are in forced or indentured labor, with a further 15 million in forced marriages, according to the International Labour Organization.

However, unlike during the historical slave trade, such arrangements are now illegal in many countries across the world, including in Sumner's native Britain, where in 2017, 2,255 slavery-related crimes were recorded. This conviction rate suggests that Sumner may come to regret his casual admission of owning another person, and could expect swift action against him from law enforcement. As such, the evidence leads us to one conclusion: Sumner is merely pretending to own another human being as part of an elaborate sting.

WHAT'S THE FREQUENCY, KENNETH?

REM

The effects of radio waves and electromagnetic radiation—all measured by frequency—have been the subject of debate and concern for decades: people worry their mobile phone will give them cancer, that wind turbines make them ill, or that WiFi gives them migraines.

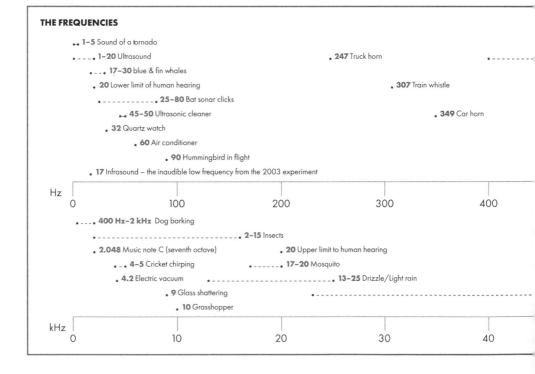

THE FREQUENCIES

1–5 Sound of a tornado

1–20 Ultrasound

17–30 blue & fin whales

20 Lower limit of human hearing

25–80 Bat sonar clicks

45–50 Ultrasonic cleaner

32 Quartz watch

60 Air conditioner

90 Hummingbird in flight

17 Infrasound – the inaudible low frequency from the 2003 experiment

247 Truck horn

307 Train whistle

349 Car horn

Hz

0   100   200   300   400

400 Hz–2 kHz Dog barking

2–15 Insects

2.048 Music note C (seventh octave)

20 Upper limit to human hearing

4–5 Cricket chirping

17–20 Mosquito

4.2 Electric vacuum

13–25 Drizzle/Light rain

9 Glass shattering

10 Grasshopper

kHz

0   10   20   30   40

It's perhaps unsurprising, then, that Stipe, M., dedicated time to working out a particular frequency that seemed to be causing him concern. The origins of Stipe's queries are unusual—his study grew out of an attack on the news anchor Dan Rather in 1986. Rather was attacked on the street by a man repeatedly shouting "Kenneth, what's the frequency?" At that point in 1994, the motives for the attack remained a complete mystery.

Based on the available information it is difficult to be certain as to what frequency Stipe is trying to find on behalf of Rather's attacker, but he describes it as "your

Benzedrine." Benzedrine is the brand name of the first pharmaceutical drug that contained amphetamines, so it's fair to assume it's a frequency that acts as a stimulant rather than a depressive.

One answer might lie in an experiment conducted in 2003 in an auditorium on London's South Bank by the National Physical Laboratory, which played an inaudible low-frequency sound alongside one of two songs across two public concerts—swapping each song between the two concerts. People at each concert reported feeling uneasy, uncomfortable, or having chills during the track where the inaudible noise was played—all markers of side effects of a stimulant like Benzedrine. This offers up a likely answer to Stipe's query: the frequency could be "infrasound," or 17 Hz.

Not long after Stipe's inquiry, the original mystery was also solved following the arrest of Rather's attacker: a mentally ill man called William Tager. He had believed television networks were transmitting signals into his mind and wanted to know how they were doing it. Tager had fatally shot an NBC stagehand outside the Rockefeller Center in 1994. NBC was broadcast on VHF channels 2–13 in the 1990s, so, though they were not broadcasting signals into Tager's brain, they were certainly operating between 54 and 216 MHz.

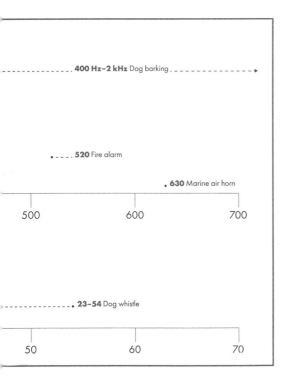

WHAT GIRLS _REALLY_ WANT

Supporting young people with their mental health   **34%**

Stopping sexual harassment   **31%**

More women in top jobs   **27%**

Tackling violence against women and girls   **27%**

Tackling discrimination against people who are
lesbian, gay, bisexual, and transgender   **26%**

Tackling the sexist objectification of women in society
(that is, where women are seen as sex objects)(13+)   **25%**

0   50   100

Percentage girls that want...

DO GIRLS JUST WANNA HAVE FUN?

CYNDI LAUPER

Modern feminism has changed the priorities and expectations of women and girls across the planet, as noted by Lauper, C.'s, seminal study into what girls want.

Lauper notes to her mother during the course of her research that "we're not the fortunate ones," accurately summarizing the current generation of women's reduced job security, wealth, and financial stability when compared with their parents.

There is also empirical evidence supporting Lauper's assertion that girls do not simply wish to settle down. An annual survey of girls carried out by the UK organization Girlguiding in 2009 found that 56 percent said marriage was the thing they would most like to achieve by age 30—but just three years later the poll found girls defined success as being "confident and independent," with only 21 percent defining it as marriage.

However, Lauper may have pushed her conclusions too far: girls want far more than merely to "have fun." The 2017 survey asked girls aged eleven to twenty-one about their priorities. The top five in the rankings were "supporting young people in their mental health," "stopping sexual harassment," "more women in top jobs," "tackling violence against women and girls," and "tackling LGBTQ discrimination."

Girls might, as Lauper cites, wanna have fun—but they also want independence, mental health services, freedom from harassment, and a strong career path, too.

WHERE DO BROKEN HEARTS GO?

WHITNEY HOUSTON

Given how much time many of us spend worrying about our romantic lives, it is of no surprise that researchers such as Houston, W., have tried to establish a good evidential basis for what happens when love goes awry (those looking for cardiological explanations should see "What Becomes of the Brokenhearted?").

One of Houston's primary concerns is whether broken hearts can "find their way home," a reference either to a new relationship or toward recovery. While there is no easy average time to record meeting a new partner, a study in the *Journal of Positive Psychology* established that the average time for recovery of normal mood following a breakup is eleven weeks—though in the instance of the end of a marriage this increases to eighteen months.

This suggests that Houston's hope that broken hearts recover are met, though not necessarily in a short period of time. Perhaps even more usefully, though, there is also data on where not to go if you want to avoid a broken heart. A survey of 2,187 people found that 1,056 had at some point broken up within six months of their first holiday with a partner—with some destinations appearing far more high risk than others. The top three pre-breakup locations were Mexico, where 21 percent of couples who visited broke up within six months, followed by Ibiza (17 percent) and Portugal (12 percent).

The best holiday destinations for those wanting to avoid heartbreak were Tenerife and Italy, the survey suggested. So perhaps inversely we can propose the answer to where broken hearts "have gone" is Mexico, Ibiza, and Portugal within the last six months.

TOP THREE DESTINATIONS FOR PEOPLE WHO HAD BROKEN UP WITHIN SIX MONTHS OF THEIR FIRST HOLIDAY TOGETHER

17% Ibiza

12% Portugal

21% Mexico

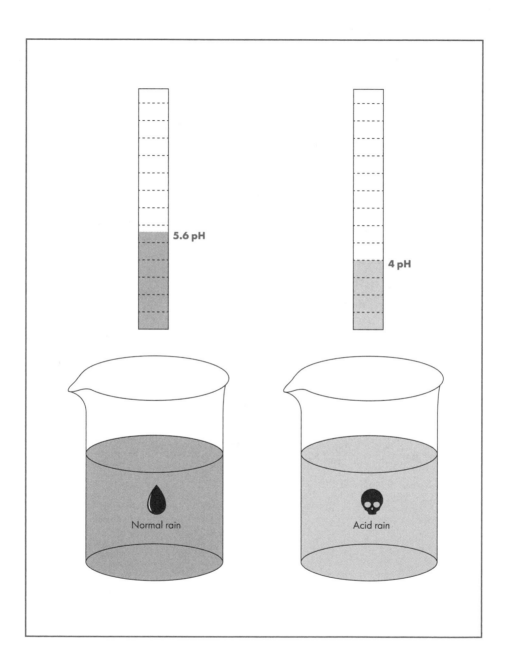

5.6 pH

4 pH

Normal rain

Acid rain

WHAT HAVE THEY DONE TO THE RAIN?

THE SEARCHERS

The research group colloquially known as "The Searchers" wondered about the effects humanity was having on rain, concerned it would not be as "gentle" as before, fearing it could burn away grass and damage the environment.

The primary concern of the Searchers in 1964, just two years after the Cuban Missile Crisis at the height of the Cold War,* was that nuclear fallout would be the source of alteration to rain, leading to widespread radiation damage. Just twenty-two years later, in 1986, the disaster at the Chernobyl nuclear power station in what is now northern Ukraine propelled vast amounts of radioactive material into the atmosphere. Rainclouds carried this material as far as the Outer Hebrides, where ten years later doctors reported massive increases of up to 2,500 percent (although this is a disputed figure) in incidences of many types of cancer. However, at the time of writing, the search for radioactive rain has proven to be in vain globally. And yet while they may have misdiagnosed the specific cause of the issue, the Searchers were correct to worry about rain generally.

They were less correct about their premise, however. Even standard, nonradioactive rain is not especially "gentle": rain is naturally acidic thanks to the carbon dioxide in the atmosphere. It has a pH of around 5.6 (pH runs from 0 to 14, where anything under 7 is acidic, and anything over is alkaline).

However, coal power plants and other sources produced sulfur dioxide, which in the atmosphere turns into a potent acid—sulfuric acid—which then rained down, causing major environmental damage. Sulfuric acid in the atmosphere changes the natural pH of rain from around 5.6 to 4.0, making it around ten times more acidic than before.

This answers the Searchers' 1964 query: "they" made the rain more acidic. Thankfully, since the 1990s, the rain has seen further developments—it is once again being made less acidic thanks to a drop in the number of coal-fired power plants. The US, for example, sees 40 percent less acidic rain than at its peak—meaning that at present we are mainly making the rain more like its natural, fairly gentle acidic state.

*The same year as the release of *Dr. Strangelove*.

SON, CAN YOU PLAY ME A MEMORY?

BILLY JOEL

In this anthropological report, Joel, B., presents a case study of an elderly man looking for help with his memory: he can recall something was "sad" and "sweet" and he knew it well when he was younger, and is hoping a piano player can help him fill in the blanks.

There is strong research evidence available on the effect of music on auditory memory—how well we remember verbal and nonverbal information that we've picked up through sounds, rather than vision or smell. This research tells us that people who play musical instruments have better auditory memory than the average person, and professional musicians have even better auditory recollection still.

However, a study in the *Psychonomic Bulletin & Review* suggests that Joel's elderly man may be pursuing a poor strategy, even if he was himself a former professional musician. The study found that visual memory is so good that even if people are shown up to 10,000 images over the course of a few hours, they can recall which they have or haven't seen with 83 percent accuracy. If shown 2,500 images they can even remember details—so, not just that they saw an apple, but which apples they did and didn't see.

The study found that even for professional musicians, auditory memory falls far short of visual memory. This does suggest a new strategy for Joel's case study, though: rather than asking Joel to play him a memory, he should ask him to show him one.

We're not quite sure what memory Joel, B., is trying to retrieve, but studies suggest it will probably have come from when he was between 16 and 25: we have a bump in autobiographical memories between those ages, known as the "reminiscence" bump. Before that, we're hit by childhood amnesia, and then memories only bump again because we're remembering things that happened more recently.

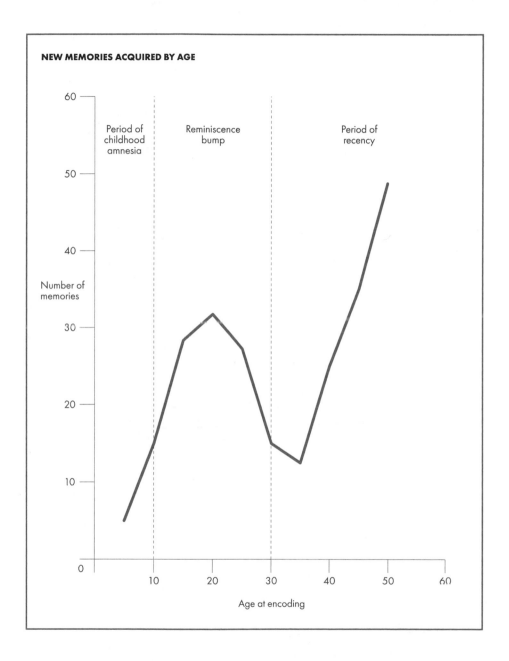

NEW MEMORIES ACQUIRED BY AGE

Period of childhood amnesia

Reminiscence bump

Period of recency

Number of memories

Age at encoding

A SELECTION OF THE TOP GOOGLED "WHY" QUESTIONS

WHY IS THE SKY BLUE?

WHY IS MY POOP GREEN?

WHY SHOULD WE HIRE YOU?

WHY ARE CATS AFRAID OF CUCUMBER?

WHY DO DOGS EAT GRASS?

WHY DO CATS PURR?

WHY DID I GET MARRIED?

WHY DO WE YAWN?

WHY DO WE DREAM?

WHY DID THE CHICKEN CROSS THE ROAD?

WHY AM I SO TIRED?

WHY AM I ALWAYS TIRED?

WHY DO CATS KNEAD?

WHY SHOULD I HIRE YOU?

WHY?

ANNIE LENNOX

It is the deceptively simple questions that often prove the most difficult to answer, as any parent who has been ambushed with "Why is the sky blue?" by their child well knows.

As such, the question provoked in this essay by Lennox, A., is perhaps the ultimate simple-to-ask and impossible-to-answer question: Why?

Thankfully, Lennox provides some cues within her essay that help direct us toward a useful answer. She notes that she may be "mad," "blind," and also "viciously unkind," but assures her correspondent that she can "still read" what they are thinking. This leads us inexorably toward a simple conclusion: Lennox believes she already knows the answer to the question she is asking, even if she is not revealing it to us.

However, we may have good reasons to question her credibility when she claims to read thoughts. A much-publicized 2011 study appeared to confirm the existence of psychic ability, or ESP, based on lab research that claimed to show students could predict whether images would appear on the left or right of a screen—apparently vindicating Lennox's claims of psychic knowledge.

However, an extensive study of 3,289 people the year after failed to replicate the results, as did another a year later. These robust studies leave us with the concern that on this issue Lennox may be an unreliable narrator.

The most frequent answers to "Why?" may also be well known to parents, though: they are in turn "because" and "because I say so."

DOES EVERYBODY WANT TO RULE THE WORLD?

TEARS FOR FEARS

It is clear that the authors of this essay, Orzabel, R., and Smith, C., have significant frustrations with the world's current governance arrangements, bemoaning "indecision" and "lack of vision" among numerous other issues.

However, the sweeping conclusion that stems from their premise—that "everybody wants to rule the world"—is one that is not remotely supported by the evidence base.

Perhaps the most powerful public office on the planet—the nearest we currently have to someone who wants to "rule the world"—is the office of US president: but most people do not aspire for their children to ever hold the role. A roundup of different polling published by Cornell University found only 32 percent of parents would want their son to pursue a career in politics, and only 34 percent would like that for their daughter.

When asked which they would rather their child be: US president, a CEO, head of a university, a sports star, or a movie star, only 7 percent chose US president—only a movie star ranked lower. Not only would many people not wish for themselves or their child to be president, they would much rather their child become a lawyer, doctor, or police officer.

Survey data published in the *Harvard Business Review* goes further still. Not only would most people not wish to rule the world, most people wouldn't even want their current boss's job: only 34 percent of US workers said they would like a leadership role, and only 7 percent wanted to be executives. Predictably, men were more likely to want to be leaders than women, though perhaps more surprisingly, African Americans and LGBTQ people were more likely to want such roles.

So, despite the bold assertions of Orzabel and Smith, most people—while they might not like how the world is going—have absolutely no intention of ruling it.

WOULD YOU RATHER YOUR CHILD BECOME PRESIDENT, OR...?

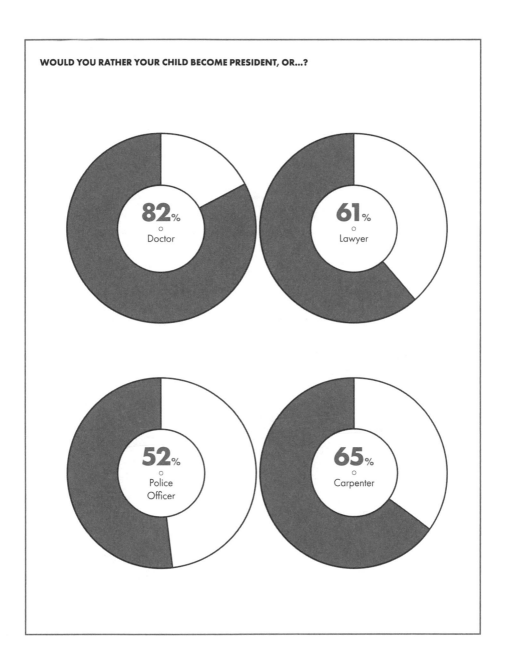

82% Doctor

61% Lawyer

52% Police Officer

65% Carpenter

HOW MANY INCHES ARE IN A MILE?

SELENA GOMEZ & THE SCENE

On the surface of it, Gomez, S., appears to be posing a very simple question here. The answer to her question can be easily obtained through Google— it is 63,360 inches. But why would this simple piece of information be enough to make someone smile?

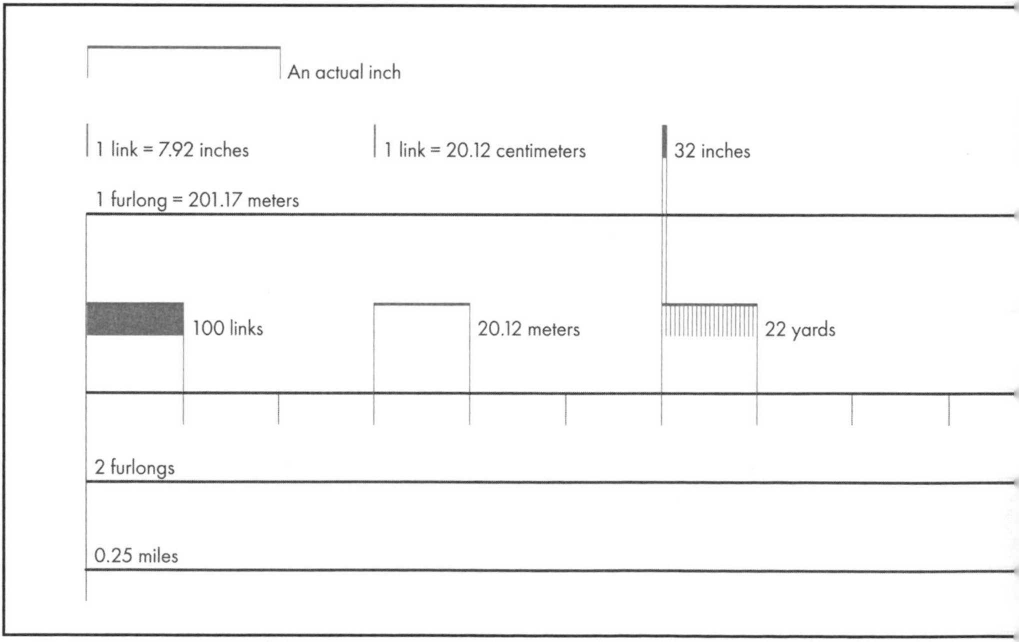

An actual inch

1 link = 7.92 inches

1 link = 20.12 centimeters

32 inches

1 furlong = 201.17 meters

100 links

20.12 meters

22 yards

2 furlongs

0.25 miles

The answer involves a series of archaic measures. The mile is a measure dating back to Roman times, and was at the time logical: one mile was defined as 1,000 paces, with paces standardized as five Roman feet—meaning one mile would be 5,000 Roman feet.

A modern mile isn't 5,000 feet, however: it is 5,280 (and each foot is 12 inches long). The reasons go back to the sixteenth century, when a mile was standardized as eight furlongs. The furlong was a useful measure as it was the maximum distance that oxen could pull a plow without needing to rest, and was standardized as 40 rods (a surveyor's tool) or 10 chains (another tool), which totals 660 feet. This measure became quite an essential one to maintain as it was used in land ownership: an acre was defined as 10 chains (one furlong) by one chain (660 feet by 66 feet).

So for simplicity, miles were defined in terms of furlongs (eight of them), which left a somewhat unmemorable set of distances to remember in the modern era. By contrast, in the metric system, a kilometer is 1,000 meters, which is in turn 100 centimeters—but 64 percent of Americans still reject the idea of switching systems. Gomez, S., is clearly talking to a proponent of the metric system in the US, who, when reminded of the illogical, piecemeal way that distance is measured under that system, allows themselves a wry smile.

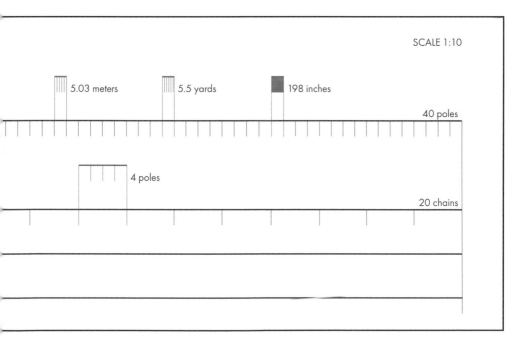

SCALE 1:10

5.03 meters   5.5 yards   198 inches

40 poles

4 poles

20 chains

HAVE GUILTY FEET GOT NO RHYTHM?

WHAM

In this meditation on fidelity and anatomy, Michael, G., postulates that as he has been unfaithful, so he wishes "never" to dance again, partly based on the premise that "guilty feet" must have no rhythm.

Given that around 10 million people in the UK—14 percent of the population—admit to having cheated, this hypothesis would explain a significant proportion of bad dancing at weddings.

However, the position does not seem to be wholly clear in this regard. In 2006, academics at the University of Manchester tried to examine the effectiveness of a range of arts and dramatic remedies on UK offenders—or, in other words, examining whether guilty feet have rhythm, and whether restoring rhythm to guilty feet would help offenders.

When it came to dance, these results were decidedly mixed: an effort to set up a dance program in a male young offenders' institute failed—researchers could find only one dance company working with male prisoners, but they were unable to start a dance program due to the lack of space for the project. For male prisoners, there was no chance for guilty feet to dance, rhythmically or otherwise.

The group did succeed in setting up a program in a women's prison, which signed up thirteen prisoners, one of whom was asked to drop out for fighting. The study didn't report the quality of the dancing, but noted that the feedback found the project an "oasis," "source of pride," and a boost of "self-belief": dance can, perhaps, be a positive.

This appears to have been the case for Michael, too: despite his pledges never to dance again, he did so, rhythmically, for decades until his death in 2016.

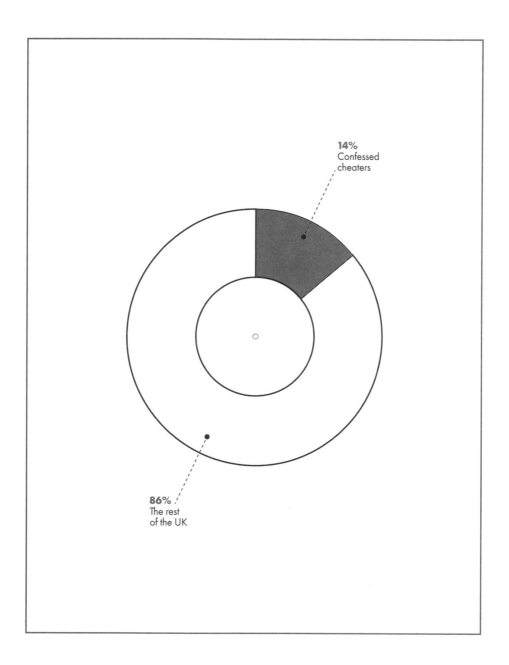

14%
Confessed
cheaters

86%
The rest
of the UK

CZECH	zmizet po anglicku	("to leave English style")
FRENCH	filer à l'anglaise	("to leave English style")
GERMAN	sich (auf) französisch empfehlen, literally einen französischen Abschied nehmen	("to take a French leave")
	or	
	einen polnischen Abgang machen	("to take a Polish leave")
HUNGARIAN	angolosan távozni	("to leave English style")
ITALIAN	andarsene all'inglese	("to leave English style")
POLISH	wyjść po angielsku	("to leave English style")
ROMANIAN	a o sterge englezeste	("to leave English style")
UKRAINIAN	піти по-англійськи (pity po-anhliys ky)	("to leave English style")
PORTUGUESE	saída à francesa	("to leave French style")
RUSSIAN	уйти по-английски (ujti po-anglijski)	("to leave English style")
SPANISH	despedida a la francesa	("goodbye in the French way," "French farewell")
WALLOON	spiter a l'inglesse	("to leave English style")
ENGLISH	Irish goodbye	

HOW THE HELL AM I SUPPOSED TO LEAVE?

USHER

Raymond, U., is seeking help for an all-too-common dilemma in modern etiquette. He is at a party and being asked to stay for another dance, but wishes to leave, and is evidently uncertain as to whether or not it's acceptable to do so, and lacks strategies to execute a quiet departure.

Such social anxieties are common, but happily there are experts in the field able to offer solutions to Raymond's issues. Much information can be found in the handbook of Britain's aristocracy, *Tatler* magazine. The outlet assures its readers that in a dinner party situation, it is acceptable to leave after dessert has been served—even if coffee has not yet been delivered. It stresses that for weddings it is not acceptable to leave before the speeches, but is otherwise silent on the issue of parties without dinner or nuptials. This leaves Raymond with enough etiquette leeway to leave if he so wishes.

In terms of executing such an exit, the magazine has a few further tips to offer—some perhaps more sincere than others.

Raymond can attempt to leave by claiming he had lost an engagement ring, hide until a major event or speech and flee, or escape via the garden, it suggests.

A more common way of leaving social situations is referred to in the UK as an "Irish goodbye": simply leaving a party without saying goodbye to anyone, so that your departure is barely noticed. In Spain and Portugal, such an exit is known as a French farewell; in Germany it's referred to as Polish leave. But in countries including France, Italy, Hungary, and Russia it's got another name: leaving English style. So, whatever the ethnic makeup of the party, it is unlikely that Raymond, U.'s, leaving without saying goodbye will be remarkable.

IS THERE LIFE ON MARS?

DAVID BOWIE

If there is an underappreciated pioneer in the field of astrobiology, then it must surely be Bowie, D., the author of the groundbreaking study "Life on Mars," published in 1971.

However eccentric Bowie's methodology might be, including encouraging a young girl to go unaccompanied to watch a film about sailors fighting in a dancehall and a policeman assaulting an innocent man, the hypothesis offered therein—that our nearest celestial neighbor may harbor life—was decades ahead of its time, and has since received corroboration from modern science.

Bowie's hypothesis received support when ice was discovered on Mars, evidencing that at least one essential requirement for life as we know it—water—was present on the planet. This briefly became more exciting still as NASA appeared to find evidence of liquid water on the planet, which would be far more likely to support life. However, in 2017 different researchers theorized the "water" was more likely to be sand, dashing those hopes.

But in 2018, the Curiosity rover on the surface of Mars uncovered something even more interesting: the kind of organic matter that would be suitable for basic life to feed on—though it can't be determined whether it came from living matter, a chemical reaction, or even something crashing into the surface of the planet.

Given that Mars used to be warmer and thus more conducive to life, one theory is that there was life on Mars, but is no longer. However, what we do know now is that if there is life on Mars, there's something there for it to eat. Bowie was onto something.

In 2011, a team of researchers led by Dirk Schulze-Makuch, of Washington State University, published an article in the journal *Astrobiology* in which they came up with an index for how friendly to life the planets were.

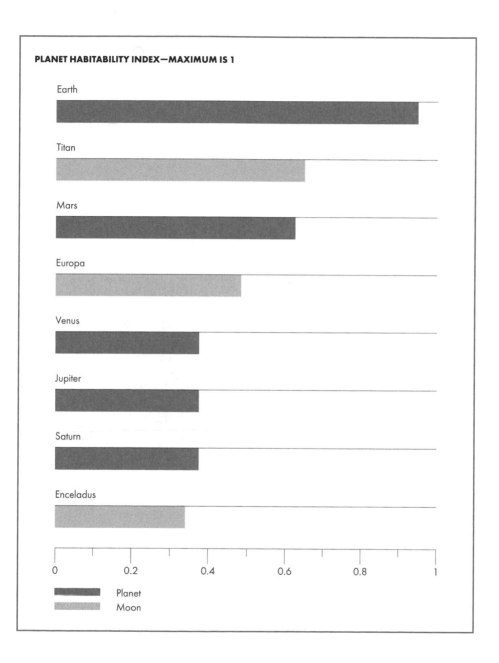

PLANET HABITABILITY INDEX—MAXIMUM IS 1

Earth

Titan

Mars

Europa

Venus

Jupiter

Saturn

Enceladus

0   0.2   0.4   0.6   0.8   1

Planet
Moon

THINGS GOING ON IN ANY GIVEN DAY

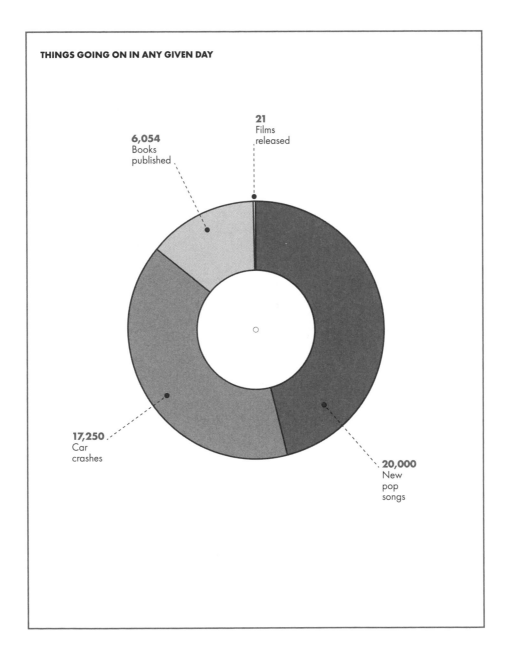

21
Films
released

6,054
Books
published

17,250
Car
crashes

20,000
New
pop
songs

WHAT'S GOING ON?

4 NON BLONDES

One cannot accuse Perry, L., and her collaborators of lacking in ambition when setting out their research question. Perry leads her cohorts in asking firmly and repeatedly, "What's going on?," but declines to offer any specificity to her inquiries: she is, it seems, interested in everything going on around her on the climb up the "great big hill of hope" that she deems life to be. *

On any given day, then, there are millions of answers to Perry's query, some of which are provided here. Across the planet there will be around 360,000 births "going on," while around 150,000 people will die. In the US around 17,250 cars will crash, resulting in around 110 fatalities. More happily, around 102,465 planes will take flight across the planet, and statistically we would expect all of them to land safely.

When it comes to creative happenings, there is no shortage there either: around 21 feature films will be released across the planet, and 6,054 books published. Apple will sell around 594,000 iPhones. Around 60 million photos will be published on Instagram, and 500 million posts will go online on Twitter.

We suspect this will be of little interest to the enlightened readership of this tome, but estimates suggest around 20,000 pop songs would be released on that given day, too. So to answer Perry's question as much as we can: there's always lots going on.

For example, on the day of the study's release, June 23, 1993, Nigeria's military dictator, General Ibrahim Babangida, annulled the results of the elections and in so doing halted the country's return to democracy, the United Nations authorized a global oil embargo on Haiti, and Lorena Gallo Bobbitt cut off her husband John Wayne Bobbitt's penis. That's enough to make anyone say "hey."

*Earlier investigations of the question by Gaye, M., limited themselves to what was going on in the specific instance of the study in late sixties America.

WHO LET THE DOGS OUT?

BAHA MEN

This anthropological exploration, published in 2000 by a sizable research collaboration in the Bahamas, informally referred to as the Baha Men, poses the question as to who released the hounds exactly twenty times.

The reason for this persistent curiosity becomes clear when we consider the history of domestication of dogs. Perhaps the closest genetic relative to modern dogs is the gray wolf; we are confident that dogs are domesticated descendants of those wolves. Because we believe they were domesticated initially to help with hunting—especially in woodland terrain—we can establish that whoever first let the dogs out was whoever first let the dogs in.

The answer to this question remains a mysterious one: the oldest generally agreed fossilized dog was discovered in 1914 in Germany (it was not examined until 1919, as people were dealing with other priorities at the time). However, new research suggests dogs were also independently domesticated in or around what is in modern times China—and eventually the two groups met and cross-mated. So while we don't know for sure which of those two groups initially let the dogs out, we have good reason to believe both groups did so.

However, the Baha Men were not specific as to which time period they were seeking to place their question, so we should also look at who is most likely to release dogs in the modern day. The answer in this instance lies with those protesting animal testing, for which thousands of dogs are used: in the US, the Rescue + Freedom Project has released about 1,000 dogs over eight years.

A much larger single release, though, occurred in India in 2016, when a lab was refused permission to use dogs for cosmetics testing, leading to 156 two- to five-year-old beagles being released—seeing the sun for the first time—before they were rehoused. In that instance, it was the Indian government and a rescue charity who let the dogs out.

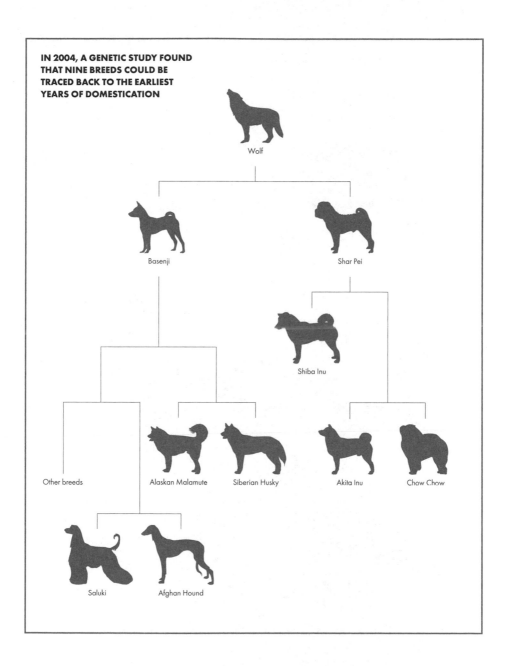

IN 2004, A GENETIC STUDY FOUND THAT NINE BREEDS COULD BE TRACED BACK TO THE EARLIEST YEARS OF DOMESTICATION

Wolf

Basenji

Shar Pei

Shiba Inu

Other breeds

Alaskan Malamute

Siberian Husky

Akita Inu

Chow Chow

Saluki

Afghan Hound

ACHILLES AND THE TORTOISE

Also known as Xeno's paradox, this involves a race between a moving tortoise with a 100-yard head start, and Achilles, who is much faster. In 10 seconds, he has closed half the distance, but the tortoise has moved fractionally further. And every 10 seconds, as he gets closer, the tortoise has moved even more fractionally ahead—meaning it's apparently impossible to ever overtake him.

THE CROCODILE PARADOX

A philosophical crocodile has stolen a child, telling its parents the child will only be returned if they correctly guess what the crocodile will do next. If the parents guess he won't return the child, we're stuck in a paradox: if he doesn't return it, then they're correct and he has to return it—making them wrong, and meaning he shouldn't return it.

THE RAVEN PARADOX

This paradox relates to epistemology: about what serves as evidence for how we know something, based on the premise that "all ravens are black" and "if something is not black, then it is not a raven." Unbelievably—this is why no one likes philosophers—this leads us to a bunch of headaches in formal logical terms.

IS THIS SONG ABOUT YOU?

(BECAUSE YOU'RE SO VAIN YOU THINK THIS SONG IS ABOUT YOU)
CARLY SIMON

Ever since it was first posited by Simon, C., in 1972, the question of whether someone was "so vain" that they believed the discussion to be about them has been broached as a classical paradox.

The reasoning goes that if the target of Simon's verbal sally believes the song to be about them then they are not vain to think so, they are merely accurate. But if they are not so vain as to think they are the target, then the song may just be wrong.

Such a situation need not, however, present a paradox as it leaves open multiple possibilities. The first is that Simon's conjecture leaves her some wiggle room, by referring to "probably" as a hedge, while the second is that Simon may simply be wrong about her target's vanity. A third possibility is that Simon has correctly identified her target as vain, but is being unfair to suggest that he is vain because of his views on the song, as his views on the song are in reality accurate.

We would like to offer a new solution to the situation. In a famous physics thought experiment, Erwin Schrödinger posited the idea of a cat shut in a box with a radioactive isotope that released poison into the box, killing the cat.

Until the box was opened, he suggested, we have no way of establishing whether the cat is alive or dead, meaning the cat is both alive and dead until the act of opening the box fixes it in one or the other state.

Simon, we venture, achieved the same with vanity. Through her act of making the target's vanity dependent on a self-defeating statement in her song, she had, in effect, discovered quantum vanity: her target is both vain and not vain, and thus a clear contribution to modern science and philosophy. It would be impossible to imagine the work of West, K., and the Kardashian lab without Simon's pioneering work on vanity.

WHAT WOULD HAPPEN IF IT WERE CHRISTMAS EVERY DAY?

WIZZARD

In this chilling and nihilistic 1973 study into the impact of redrawing the calendar so that it is Christmas every day, Wizzard was guilty of a very partial investigation into an event that would surely cause economic recession and possibly the collapse of much of the global economy. They begin from the faulty premise that, it being Christmas, every day would somehow mean a state of perpetual winter in which their favored snow-related recreation would continue. But even putting aside this inaccuracy, they leave out many of the massive downsides.

As Wizzard was surely fully aware, in most of the Western world almost all shops and workplaces are required by law to close for the day, an act which, if repeated daily, would quickly cause shortfalls of food and other essential supplies—though in the short run greatly increase the profits and returns of the few shops allowed and able to open. The result of this would be to very quickly force a battle of civilizations between those who celebrate Christmas and those who do not, as one fed economically on the other.

The disastrous economic backlash as people eventually stopped receiving salaries, unless they were members of the noncelebrating Christmas service provision, would be heightened by the social requirements of the day: Christmas is seen by many to require lavish feasting and the exchange of gifts. Without such elements, they would feel it was no longer "Christmas every day." We could thus expect to see turkeys and other feasting birds slaughtered to extinction, before people moved on to wild animals, household pets, and potentially each other, while civil law would break down as people constantly hunted for new, daily gifts for their loved ones. Eventually, "gifts" would become what could be stolen or taken by force from others.

Finally, the mental health implications of every day spent with extended family is impossible to compute and would surely lead to total societal breakdown within a matter of months. The only bells ringing out in this terrifying alternate future would be those of the corpse bearers as they made their way through desolate burning streets.

CURRENT ONE-DAY CHRISTMAS CONSUMPTION IN THE UK

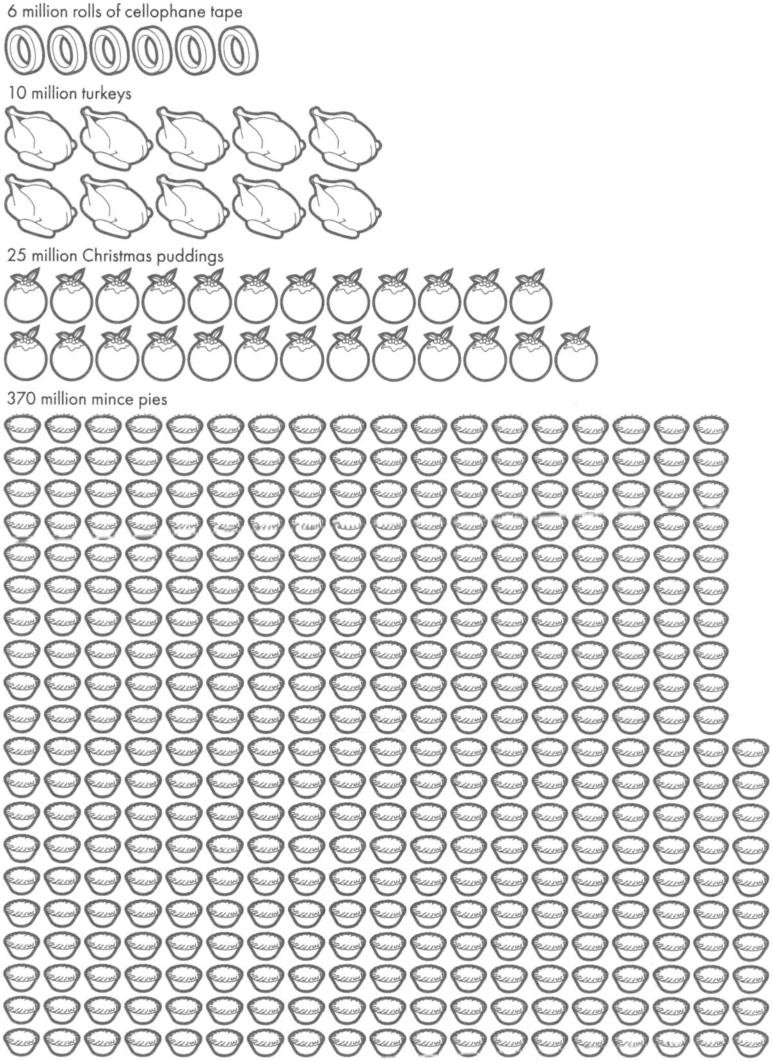

6 million rolls of cellophane tape

10 million turkeys

25 million Christmas puddings

370 million mince pies

IF BIRDS DO SUDDENLY APPEAR, WHAT YOU SHOULD CALL THEM		**A** A weight of albatrosses	**B** A bellowing of bullfinches
C A murder of crows	**D** A dole of doves	**E** A congress of eagles	**F** A charm of finches
G A skein of geese	**H** A siege of herons	**I**	**J** A clattering of jackdaws
K	**L** An exaltation of larks	**M** A mischief of magpies	**N** A watch of nightingales
O A parliament of owls	**P** A pandemonium of parrots	**Q** A bevy of quail	**R** An unkindness of ravens
S A quarrel of sparrows	**T** A mutation of thrushes	**U**	**V** A venue of vultures
W A descent of woodpeckers	**X**	**Y** An incontinence of yellowlegs	**Z**

WHY DO BIRDS SUDDENLY APPEAR?

THE CARPENTERS

The brother-and-sister team behind this flawed project deserves a measure of praise for accurately identifying a phenomenon long before mainstream science, but this must be tempered by their poor attribution of its cause.

Carpenter, K., and Carpenter, R., accurately identified that the movement of birds has become less predictable, causing them at times to "suddenly appear." Unfortunately—and with little evidence given in their discourse—they attribute this to the birds wishing to be "close to" the Carpenters' subject. As they state that, in this desire, the birds are "just like me," it suggests both Carpenters are experiencing a severe case of projection—wrongly ascribing their own motivations to others—for which they may need to seek appropriate help.

Thankfully, recent science offers a more solid explanation for the unpredictable arrival of birds—especially as it relates to their migratory patterns. A 2017 paper in the *Scientific Reports* journal notes that migrating birds aim to arrive in a new region just as "green-up" occurs, i.e., when the first shoots from buds appear—but due to climate change multiple species are now missing that time, often by several days.

Another paper in the same journal notes that artificial light at night is further disrupting migration patterns. The papers note that the consequences of this random timing can be severe, leading to die-outs in the bird population and thus spiraling populations of some insect pests, disrupting crop production. If more attention had been paid to the Carpenters' initial, if flawed, observation, perhaps these consequences could have been avoided.

The study's further claims that such logic can also be applied to stars in the sky and girls around town and that this is down to angels applying liberal amounts of moondust and starlight are less easy to validate, though do perhaps point to an apprehension that light is to blame where the birds are concerned.

WHAT IF GOD WAS ONE OF US?

JOAN OSBORNE

In her classic 1995 thought experiment, theologian Osborne, J., pondered what would happen if God manifested on Earth as one of us. Her investigation includes what his name would be, whether you would say it to his face, and what single question you would ask him.

Given that the idea of God varies between cultures and religions, we would expect his manifestation to be vastly different depending on which culture's idea of God (if any) were correct. And even if we limit ourselves to the Judeo-Christian conception of God, there are more than twenty different ways that God is addressed at different points in the Bible, including El, Eloah Adonai, and Yahweh. As to whether you could say it to his face—in Genesis 32:30 Jacob claims he has "seen God face to face," but in John 1:18 it says, "No Man hath seen God at any time." Moses is made to stand on a big rock, so he can't see God.

However, it is most likely that Osborne is referring to the concept of God appearing in the form of a man, as Christian believers maintain he did through the body of Jesus. This is backed up by Osborne's encouragement to imagine him as a "slob on a bus" trying to get home. Many conceptions of Jesus would fit this description.

Leaving aside the obvious issue that if you are on a bus going to heaven, you should probably remain quiet and hope you arrive, it's worth thinking about the questions that Osborne cleverly does not pose. Given most religions pose God as omniscient, he would already know what question you were going to ask whether or not you asked it, so in effect you do not need to ask the question.

Indeed, all questions asked by everyone are eternally present in his head, so, as Osborne is clearly suggesting, God being one of us would in no way change anything. An infinite variety of every question possible to ask would exist in the permanent now of his consciousness, whatever you do.

Osborne does, however, risk a serious schism in the Catholic church by suggesting that the Pope calls God on a phone. If so, the question we should probably ask God is, "What's your number?"

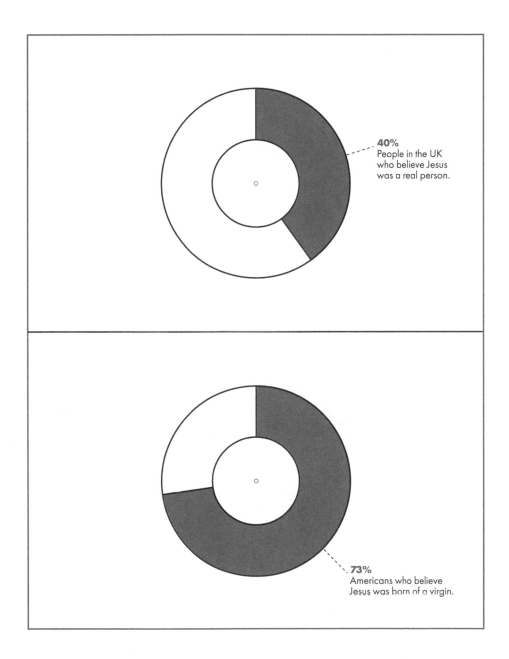

40%
People in the UK
who believe Jesus
was a real person.

73%
Americans who believe
Jesus was born of a virgin.

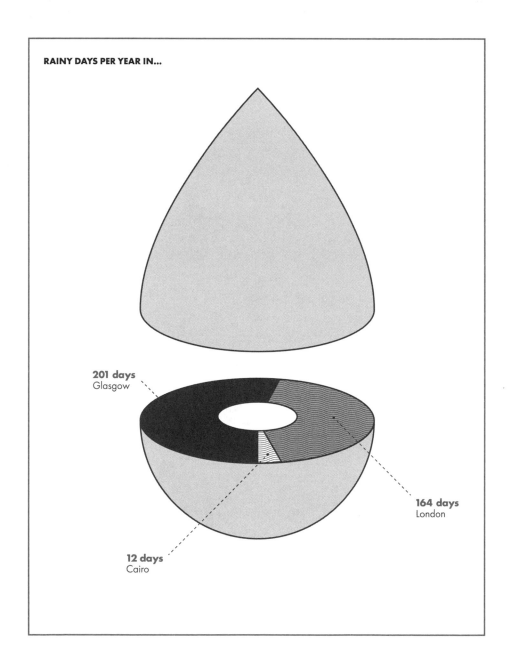

RAINY DAYS PER YEAR IN...

201 days
Glasgow

164 days
London

12 days
Cairo

WHY DOES IT ALWAYS RAIN ON ME?

TRAVIS

Healy, F., and his collaborators on this work demonstrate remarkably unusual priorities here, focusing almost entirely on why they are so frequently subject to rain, ignoring their own stated insomnia and their difficulties caused by lightning.

Given their focus on the question of why they are so regularly exposed to rain, it is fitting that we tackle this question first. Perhaps, ironically, it is by looking at which professions are most likely to be exposed to the sun that we could see who would be outside—and therefore subject to being rained upon.

The *British Journal of Cancer* did exactly this in a study of melanomas, finding the professions most at risk thanks to their outdoor work were construction workers, followed by agriculture workers, followed by police and armed services. We can therefore assume Healy et al. were looking at such a worker.

If that worker was in their hometown of Glasgow, this would further explain the rain: because of their proximity to the Atlantic Ocean, the west of Scotland and Ireland are subject to particularly high rainfall.

However, we feel the more pressing issue for Healy is that he "can't avoid the lightning." In normal circumstances there would be much Healy could do to increase his chances of avoiding lightning, including not sheltering under trees, taking cover indoors if possible, or even better in a car, where the metal shell and rubber tires would leave him very safe. However, if Healy is plagued by regular lightning even when the sun shines, he may wish to present himself to authorities, who could take advantage of his misfortune to generate cheap power.

There are no known correlations between lying—at seventeen or any other age—and average rainfall, or its consequences. Unless the lie he told when he was seventeen was, "Yes, I do have an umbrella and full set of waterproof clothing, thank you."

WHO DO YOU THINK YOU ARE?

SPICE GIRLS

This seminal neurological exploration from a group of five—Adams, V., Brown, M., Bunting, E., Chisholm, M., and Halliwell, G.,—examines our sense of self-identity, including where it comes from and what preserves it.

Other work alongside has helped to answer the question posed, at least in part, by establishing that our sense of self-identity comes from the brain: it is believed to be related to the activity of the right frontal lobe, according to research on seventy-two patients presented to the American Academy of Neurology.

A study of patients suffering a rare form of dementia affecting that region found that people's identity occasionally changed as a result of the condition. While some primarily had issues with forgetting the identities of loved ones, others' sense of who they were changed more dramatically. A sexually conservative and risk-averse man became a liberated job-hopper, while another woman ditched designer attire and fine dining for casual and fast food. Elsewhere, people have spontaneously developed foreign accents— even never having visited the country in question.

While the collaboration—known as SPICE, though we were unable to source the origin of this acronym—raised questions as to how our brains maintain our sense of activity, their medical advice was accurate. They advised to "swing," "shake," "move," and "make"—all examples of regular physical exercise, which is believed to significantly lower the risk of dementia.

THE PREDICTED NUMBER OF PEOPLE WITH DEMENTIA WORLDWIDE

2017

50 million
people with
dementia.

2030

82 million
people with
dementia.

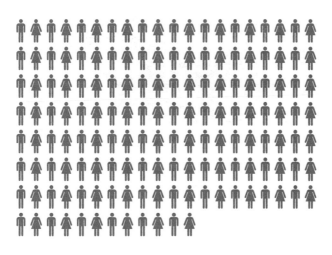

2050

152 million
people with
dementia.

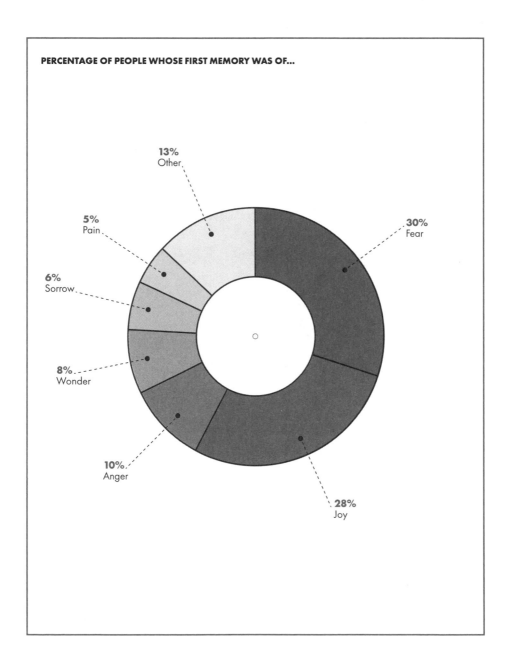

PERCENTAGE OF PEOPLE WHOSE FIRST MEMORY WAS OF...

13% Other

5% Pain

6% Sorrow

8% Wonder

10% Anger

28% Joy

30% Fear

DO YOU REMEMBER THE FIRST TIME?

PULP

Cocker, J., and his collaborators introduce thought-provoking musings on the nature of memory in their 1994 project. When it comes to whether we remember the first time we did some things—walked, perhaps, or ate solid food, the answer is no.

For many of us, our first memory is a hazy thing, usually from around the age of three or four. This is because of a phenomenon known as "childhood amnesia," which leaves most of us with virtually no memories before the age of three, and relatively few from before the age of ten, when compared to the rest of our lives.

Studies have found this effect is gradual: during childhood, we can apparently recall some events back to around the age of one—though some psychologists speculate this could be children recalling events as described more recently by others—only then to lose memory of them later.

However, if Cocker et al. are looking into sibling birth or hospitalization, evidence has shown memory of these events can persist despite childhood amnesia, to an extent. Research suggests that a recollection of these significant events can sustain from the age of two.

One alternative hypothesis posits that Cocker et al. are in fact researching recollection of the first time someone slept with them. Most of us can recall this, though many of us would rather not: 58 percent of US adults said their first time sleeping with their current partner was "awkward" or "terrible."

WHO STARTED THE FIRE?

BILLY JOEL

In this discourse, Joel, B., is especially keen that we absolve him and anyone associated with him of having been the originator of fire—claiming instead that it has always been burning, "since the world's been turning." Joel's claim is not without merit, but requires some scrutiny.

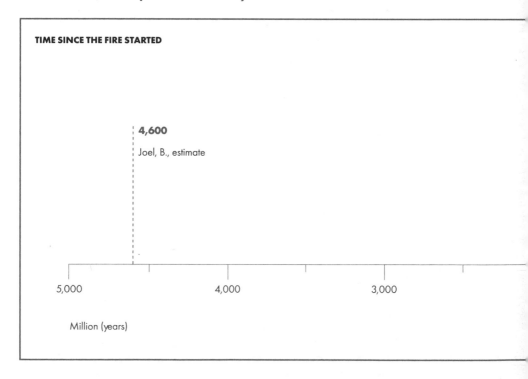

TIME SINCE THE FIRE STARTED

4,600
Joel, B., estimate

5,000   4,000   3,000

Million (years)

Joel is correct to dismiss cosmological events such as the Big Bang and even the activity of the sun from his analysis, as neither are strictly fire: one was the expansion of matter, and the other is a nuclear fusion reaction. Fire, instead, is the reaction of flammable materials with oxygen in the atmosphere.

However, Joel is wrong to say things have been burning since the world was turning. When the Earth formed, around 4.6 billion years ago, it was already turning, but lacked enough oxygen in its atmosphere to start a fire.

A combustible material such as wood will only ignite if the atmosphere has 15–17 percent oxygen in it, which has been the case for less than 850 million years. In this sense, Joel is correct that humans did not start the first fires on Earth, but his timeline is off by nearly 4 billion years.

As to Joel's second claim—that even if we collectively did not start the fire, we have "tried to fight it"—he may be on fairly solid ground here. Across most developed countries, around one in 1,000 of the population is employed as a firefighter, while the remainder of the population contributes to this effort through taxation.

Despite Joel's advocacy, "It was always burning" is not recommended as a defense in an arson trial.

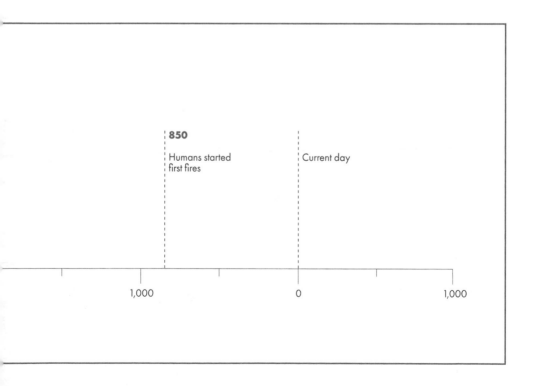

850

Humans started first fires

Current day

1,000   0   1,000

A NOTE ON CITATIONS

Where we've made significant use of a particular study or article, we've included it wherever possible in the text. However, to avoid a notes section as long as the book itself, these have sometimes been omitted. If there's any figure you'd like the source of—or if you think you've spotted an error in the math—do get in touch, ideally via Twitter, where I can be found @jamesrbuk.

SONG
CREDITS

SONG TITLE	WRITING CREDITS	PUBLISHING RIGHTS
BLOWIN' IN THE WIND	Bob Dylan	Bob Dylan Music obo Special Rider MusicDo
KILLING ME SOFTLY	Norman Gimbel, Charles Fox	Warner-Tamerlane Pub Co. obo Rodali Music/Words West LLC
A DAY IN THE LIFE	John Lennon, Paul McCartney	Sony/ATV Tunes LLC dba ATV obo ATV (Northern Songs Catalog)
(HOW MUCH IS) THAT DOGGIE IN THE WINDOW?	Bob Merrill	Music & Media Int'l obo Golden Bell Songs
DO THEY KNOW IT'S CHRISTMAS? (FEED THE WORLD)	Midge Ure, Bob Geldof	WB Music Corp. obo Chappell Music Ltd.
HOW SOON IS NOW?	Johnny Marr, Steven Morrissey	Universal-Polygram Int'l obo Marr Songs Ltd./Warner Tamerlane Pub Corp./B/O Muziekuitgeverij Artemis BV
CAN I KICK IT?	Lou Reed	EMI Blackwood Music Inc. obo Oakfield Avenue Music Ltd.
MS. JACKSON	Andre Benjamin, Antwan Patton, David Sheats	BMG Monarch/EMI April Music Inc.
LADY MARMALADE	Robert Crewe, Kenny Nolan	Stone Diamond Music Corp. obo Tannyboy Music Co./Jobete Music Co. obo Kenny Nolan Publishing
RUN THE WORLD (GIRLS)	Thomas Wesley Pentz, Beyoncé Knowles, Dave Taylor, Terius Nash, Adidja Azim Palmer, Nick Van De Wall	EMI April Music Inc. obo B-Day Publishing/ WB Music Corp. obo 2082 Music Publishing/ NW Collections obo Jack Russell Music Ltd./ Kobalt Music Pub America Inc./Stemra/ Copyright Control N EMI April Music Inc./ EMI April Music Inc. obo Switch Werd Music
ETERNAL FLAME	Susanna Lee Hoffs, Thomas F. Kelly, William E. Steinberg	Songs of Universal obo Bangophile Music/ Sony/ATV Tunes LLC

WAR	Barrett Strong, Norman Whitfield	EMI Blackwood Music Inc. obo Stone Agate Music
UMBRELLA	Thaddis Laphonia Harrell, Shawn Carter, Christopher A. Stewart, Terius Youngdell Nash	Sony/ATV Tunes LLC obo Samp-Uk Ltd./WB Music Corp./WB Music Corp. obo Carter Boys Music/WB Music Corp. obo 2082 Music Publishing/Songs of Peer, Ltd./Songs of Peer, Ltd. obo March Ninth Music
BOHEMIAN RHAPSODY	Queen	EMI Glenwood Music Corp. obo Queen Music Ltd.
THAT'S NOT MY NAME	Jules De Martino, Katie White	WB Music Corp. obo Playwrite Music Limited/Sony/ATV Tunes LLC obo Samp-Uk Ltd.
CRY ME A RIVER	Arthur Hamilton	Chappell & Co.
WHERE HAVE ALL THE FLOWERS GONE?	Peter Seeger	Figs. D Music Inc. obo Sanga Music/Figs. D Music Inc.
SHOULD I STAY OR SHOULD I GO?	Samuel Reinhard, Joe Strummer, Mick Jones	Universal-Polygram Intl Pub obo Nineden, Ltd.
DOES YOUR MOTHER KNOW?	Aleksej Anatolevich Kortnev, Bjoern K. Ulvaeus, Benny Goran Bror Andersson	EMI Grove Park Music obo Union Songs A.B./Universal-Polygram Int'l obo Union Songs Musikforlag AB
FEVER	John Davenport, Eddie Cooley	Trio Music Co., Inc./Fort Knox Music, Inc.
I'D DO ANYTHING FOR LOVE (BUT I WON'T DO THAT)	James Richard Steinman	Edward B. Marks Music Co.
ARE "FRIENDS" ELECTRIC?	Gary Webb (Pak: Gary Numan)	Universal-Polygram Int'l Pub Inc.
MARIA	Richard Rodgers, Oscar Hammerstein II	Rodgers & Hammerstein Org.
YEAR 3000	Steve Robson, James Bourne, Mattiesargeant, Math Jay, Charlie Simpson, Matthew Fletcher	Almo Music Corp. obo Rondor Music (London) Ltd./Copyright Control
WHEN WILL I BE FAMOUS?	The Brothers	Copyright Control/Chappell & Co., Inc. obo Graham Music Pub
HUMAN	Mark August Stoermer, Dave Brent Keuning, Brandon Flowers, Ronnie Vannucci Jr.	Universal-Polygram Int'l Pub obo Universal Music Pub Ltd.

I'M GONNA BE (500 MILES)	Charles S. Reid, Craig M. Reid	WB Music Corp. obo Warner Bros. Music Ltd.
ONCE IN A LIFETIME	Brian Eno, Chris Frantz, David Byrne, Jerry Harrison, Tina Weymouth	Rhino/Warner Bros.
JERUSALEM	William Blake, Hubert Parry	Public domain
OUT OF THE WOODS	Taylor Swift, Jack Antonoff	Sony/ATV Tree Publishing obo Taylor Swift Music
I WILL SURVIVE	Dino Fekaris, Frederick J. Perren	Universal-Polygram International Pub Inc./Universal-Polygram Int'l Pub obo Perren-Vibes Music Inc.
THE CHAIN	Lindsey Buckingham, Christine McVie, Stephanie Nicks, Mick Fleetwood, John McVie	Universal Music-Careers/Reach Music Publishing
TURNING JAPANESE	David Fenton	EMI Glenwood Music Corporation
SMOOTH CRIMINAL	Michael Joe Jackson	Sony/ATV Songs LLC (non-rep) Mijac Music
INDEPENDENT WOMEN (PT 1)	Beyoncé Knowles, Cory Rooney, Samuel Barnes, Jean-Claude Olivier	Columbia Records
IS SHE REALLY GOING OUT WITH HIM?	Joe Jackson	Kobalt Music Pub America obo Pokazuka LLC
AMERICAN PIE	Don McLean	Songs of Universal, Inc. obo Benny Bird Co., Inc.
CAN YOU FEEL THE LOVE TONIGHT?	Tim Rice, Elton John	Wonderland Music Co., Inc.
CALL ME, MAYBE?	Carly Rae Jepsen, Joshua Keeler Ramsay, Tavish Joseph Crowe	Universal Music Corp. obo Jepsen Music Pub/BMG Gold Songs obo Crowe Music Inc.
FAIRYTALE OF NEW YORK	Jeremy Max Finer, Shane Patrick, Lysaght Macgowan	Universal Music MGB Songs obo Universal Music Pub MGB Ltd./ Universal-Polygram obo Universal Music Pub Ltd.
MONEY	Roger Waters	Hampshire House Publishing
WHY DON'T WE DO IT IN THE ROAD?	Lennon, McCartney	Sony/ATV Tunes LLC dba ATV obo ATV (Northern Songs Catalog)
THE DRUGS DON'T WORK	R. Ashcroft	EMI Music Publishing

NINE MILLION BICYCLES	Mike Batt	Sony/ATV Tunes LLC obo Dramatico Music Publishing Ltd.
DO YOU KNOW THE WAY TO SAN JOSÉ?	Hal David, Burt F. Bacharach	BMG Gold Songs obo Casa David Lp/ BMG Gold Songs obo New Hidden Valley Music Co.
EYE OF THE TIGER	Jim Peterik, Frank Sullivan	Sony/ATV Melody obo Rude Music/ WB Music Corp. obo Easy Action Music
WOULD I LIE TO YOU?	M. Leeson, P. Vale	BMG Platinum Songs obo BMG VM Music Ltd.
9 TO 5	Dolly Parton	Velvet Apple Music
WHAT BECOMES OF THE BROKENHEARTED?	William Weatherspoon, James Dean, Paul Riser	Stone Agate Music Corp/Jobete Music Co., Inc.
BLAME IT ON THE BOOGIE	Thomas Meyer, Hans Kampschroer, Elmar Krohn, Michael George Jackson, Rich David John Jackson	Chrysalis Music obo Edition Delay/Gema
SIGNS	Calvin Broadus, Lonnie Simmons, Pharrell Williams, Charles K. Wilson, Rudy Taylor, Chad Hugo	EMI Blackwood Music Inc. obo My Own Chit Music/Universal Music-Careers/EMI Blackwood Music Inc./Warner Geo Met Tric Music/BMG Platinum Songs obo Minder Music
CREEP	Mike Hazelwood, Albert Hammond, Jonathan Richard, Guy Greenwood, Thomas Edward Yorke, Colin Charles Greenwood, Philip James Selway, Edward John O'Brien	EMI April Music Inc./WB Music Corp. obo Warner/Chappell Music Ltd.
WHITE CHRISTMAS	Irving Berlin	Irving Berlin Music Co.
EARTH SONG	Michael Jackson	Sony/ATV Songs LLC (non-rep) Mijac Music
NOTHING COMPARES 2 U	Prince	Universal Music Corp. obo Controversy Music
ESCAPE	Rupert Holmes	WB Music Corp.
ARE YOU LONESOME TONIGHT?	Roy Turk, Lou Handman	Bourne Co./Cromwell Music
THE FOX	Tor Hermansen, Nicholas Boundy, Vegard Ylvisaaker, Mikkel Eriksen, Christian Lochstoer, Baard Ylvisaaker	EMI Blackwood Music Inc. obo Stellar Songs Ltd./EMI April Music Inc. obo EMI Music Publishing, Ltd.

IRONIC	Glen Ballard, Alanis Nadine Morissette	Songs of Universal, Inc./Songs of Universal, Inc. obo Vanhurst Place Music/Penny Farthing Music obo Arlovol Music
WHAT IS LOVE?	Junior Torello, Dee Dee Halligan	WB Music Corp. obo Hanseatic Musikverlag GMBH/Gema
LONELY THIS CHRISTMAS	M. Chapman, N. Chinn	Universal Music MGB Songs
COMPLICATED	Carolyn Dawn Johnson, Shaye Smith	EMI Blackwood Music Inc./EMI Full Keel Music Co.
ALL MY FRIENDS	James Murphy	Kobalt Music Pub America obo Guy with Head and Arms Music
HEY YA	Andre Benjamin	BMG Monarch obo Gnat Booty Music/ BMG Monarch
WHY'D YOU ONLY CALL ME WHEN YOU'RE HIGH?	Jamie Cook, Matt Helders, Nick O'Malley, Alex Turner	Domino Recording Co.
24 HOURS FROM TULSA	Burt Bacharach, Hal David	Gusto Records
EVERY BREATH YOU TAKE	Sting	EMI Blackwood Music Inc. obo Magnetic Publishing Ltd.
WHAT'S THE FREQUENCY, KENNETH?	John Michael Stipe, Peter Lawrence Buck, William Thomas Berry, Michael E. Mills	Universal Tunes obo Night Garden Music
GIRLS JUST WANT TO HAVE FUN	Robert Hazard	Sony/ATV Tunes LLC
WHERE DO BROKEN HEARTS GO?	Wildhorn, Jackson	Sony/ATV Tunes LLC/Chrysalis Music Group Inc. Digital Only
WHAT HAVE THEY DONE TO THE RAIN?	Malvina Reynolds	Nancy Schimmel dba Schroder Music Co.
PIANO MAN	Billy Joel	Almo Music Corp. obo Joelsongs
WHY?	Annie Lennox	Universal Music MGB Songs
EVERYBODY WANTS TO RULE THE WORLD	Chris Hughes, Ian Stanley, Roland Orzabal	BMG Platinum Songs obo BMG 10 Music Ltd./BMG Platinum Songs obo BMG VM Music Ltd.
TELL ME SOMETHING I DON'T KNOW	Antonina Armato, Michael David Nielsen, Ralph Nero Churchwell IV	Universal Music Corp. obo Warner Olive Music LLC/Downtown DLJ Songs LLC obo Antonina Songs

CARELESS WHISPER	George Michael, Andrew Ridgeley	WB Music Corp. obo Wham Music Limited (Gb 2)/WB Music Corp. obo Warner/Chappell MLM Limited
YEAH!	La Marquis Jefferson, Sean Garrett, James Phillips, Jonathan Smith, Christopher Bridges, Patrick Smith	Reservoir 416/EMI April Music Inc. obo Air Control Music/BMG Bumblebee obo Me and Marq Music/EMI April Music Inc. obo Basajamba Music/Songs of Windswept Pacific Y EMI April Music Inc./EMI April Music Inc. obo Ludacris Music Pub/Music of Windswept
LIFE ON MARS	David Bowie	Chrysalis Music Group Inc. Digital Only/Tintoretto Music/EMI Music Publishing Ltd.
WHAT'S UP?	Linda Perry	Sony/ATV Harmony/Sony/ATV Harmony obo Stuck in the Throat Music
WHO LET THE DOGS OUT?	Anslem D. Douglas, Osbert Leopold Gurley	BMG Platinum Songs/BMG Platinum Songs obo Hyckryck Music Pub, Inc./Wyz Girl Ent. Consulting LLC
YOU'RE SO VAIN	Carly Simon	Universal Music Corp. obo C'est Music
I WISH IT COULD BE CHRISTMAS EVERY DAY	Roy Wood	Parlophone UK
(THEY LONG TO BE) CLOSE TO YOU	Hal David, Burt F. Bacharach	BMG Gold Songs obo Casa David LP/BMG Gold Songs obo New Hidden Valley Music Co.
ONE OF US	Eric Bazilian	Universal/Island Def Jam
WHY DOES IT ALWAYS RAIN ON ME?	Francis Healy	Sony/ATV Songs LLC obo Samp-UK Ltd.
WHO DO YOU THINK YOU ARE?	Wilson, Watkins, Halliwell	Universal Music MGB Songs obo 19 Music Ltd./EMI Full Keel Music Co.
DO YOU REMEMBER THE FIRST TIME?	Nick Banks, Jarvis Cocker, Candida Doyle, Steve Mackey, Russell Senior	Universal-Island Music, Inc.
WE DIDN'T START THE FIRE	Billy Joel	Almo Music Corp. obo Joelsongs

Note: Credits sourced from HFA Songfile.